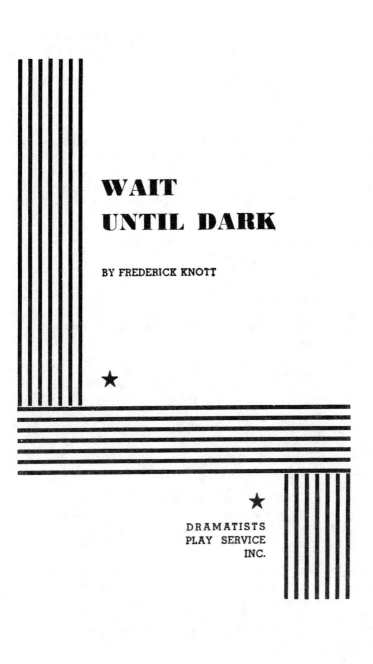

WAIT UNTIL DARK

BY FREDERICK KNOTT

★

★

DRAMATISTS
PLAY SERVICE
INC.

WAIT UNTIL DARK was first presented by Fred Coe at the Ethel Barrymore Theatre, in New York City, on February 2, 1966. It was directed by Arthur Penn; the scenery was designed and lighted by George Jenkins; and the costumes were by Ruth Morley. The cast, in order of appearance, was as follows:

MIKE TALMAN	Mitchell Ryan
SGT. CARLINO	Val Bisoglio
HARRY ROAT, JR.	Robert Duvall
SUSY HENDRIX	Lee Remick
SAM HENDRIX	James Congdon
GLORIA	Julie Herrod
POLICEMEN	William Jordan
	Richard Kuss

SYNOPSIS OF SCENES

The action takes place in a basement apartment in Greenwich Village.

ACT I

SCENE 1 Friday evening.
SCENE 2 Saturday afternoon.
SCENE 3 Twenty minutes later.

ACT II

SCENE 1 About an hour later.
SCENE 2 A few minutes later.
SCENE 3 A minute later.

'Scene 2 and Scene 3 may be combined. See note at end of Act II,
~.)

3

DESCRIPTION OF THE SET

A basement apartment in an old house in Greenwich Village.

In the left wall (stage left) are two windows. They are *high up* in the wall. They have bars outside. Inside are Venetian blinds and there is a complete *blackout* arrangement of some sort which can cover both windows (i.e. when Sam wants to use this *whole* room as his darkroom).

On the left, underneath the windows, are the sink, kitchen closets, etc. In the corner, up left, is an old refrigerator. Down left is an old washer-dryer. Back centre is Sam's photographer's working bench, with photographic equipment, drawers, filing cabinet, etc. Center of Sam's bench is a lamp (goose-neck type). It can be operated from both the light switch by bedroom door and at the lamp itself. (See, in particular II-1, and II-3.) On wall, above washer is a clock (which Susy can *feel*). In corner, up right, is a short flight of stairs leading up to the *hall door* (which is the only entrance to this apartment). This door leads to a hall-passage (street level) which leads stage right to back door, left to street door. Under the stairs is a closet. In wall, above right end of Sam's bench is a fuse-box.

In the right wall is a door which leads, off, to the bedroom and bathroom. Down right is a heavy steel safe, but this is camouflaged (i.e. with a cloth of some kind or simple facade, so as to make it look more like a chest). Over the safe, on the wall, hangs a mirror. Left centre is a kitchen table with wooden chairs. There is a small vase of flowers and a telephone on the table. Right center is a settee, with one side table and a coffee table in front of it.

The furniture is mostly inexpensive second-hand stuff, bought and re-painted by Sam. The general appearance of the room is masculine and practical.

WAIT UNTIL DARK

ACT I

SCENE 1

TIME: *Friday evening.*

DESCRIPTION OF SETS: (*see separate notes*)

ON RISE: *The stage is dark except for lighting coming through the Venetian blinds (which are open) and light from under the hall door. (The hall lights are on outside.) The bedroom door is closed. The old refrigerator is humming loudly. There is complete silence for several seconds and then we hear the back door open and close quietly, Off right. A few moments later there are two soft knocks on the hall door and Mike enters. He immediately closes door and looks around the room, suspecting that someone may already be there.*

MIKE. (*Very quietly.*) Hullo? (*After listening a moment he comes down the stairs. The refrigerator noise cuts out. Mike turns abruptly, then he continues downstairs to bedroom door and knocks quietly. No reply. He turns the handle cautiously and disappears into bedroom. We hear him Off, as he opens the bathroom door and switches light on and off and rattles a closet door. Then we hear him open and then close the bedroom drapes. At the same time, while Mike is in bedroom, we hear the back door open and close [but with more noise this time]. Then the hall doorbell rings once. The bedroom door closes quickly and a key is turned in the lock. The hall door opens and Carlino enters. He stands for a moment framed in the open doorway and listens. Then he examines the spring lock, pushing the tongue in and out. He slips the catch to lock it and closes door. He comes down to foot of stairs. He switches on the light [by bedroom door] and looks quickly around the room. Noticing the Venetian blinds are open he switches off light. He is about to try the bedroom door but, on second thoughts, he takes out his "brass knuckles" from his right pocket and puts them on, then he turns the handle and rattles it. Finding it locked*

5

he crosses L. *and pulls the cords of the Venetian blinds so they are closed over both windows. While he is doing this Mike unlocks bedroom door and enters quietly. Carlino hears this and turns sharply. Then suddenly panicking, he rushes for the stairs, snatching up a kitchen chair as he goes. He is about to throw it at Mike as he passes. Mike, sharply:*) Hold it! (*Then gently.*) Hold it—hold it . . . (*Carlino recognizes him and Mike takes the chair out of his hands.*) (*Author's Note: The above action [from Rise] must not be played too slowly.*)

CARLINO. *You!* (*Carlino switches on lights by bedroom door. Mike looks him up and down and replaces the chair where it came from.*)

MIKE. Well! I think you put on weight! . . . They paroled me three months ago—been looking for you everywhere. (*Carlino looks around the room.*)

CARLINO. This your place?

MIKE. *My* place!

CARLINO. When did you move in here? (*As he obviously believes it, Mike decides to kid him along.*)

MIKE. I—er—about a month ago.

CARLINO. Photography! Who taught you all this?

MIKE. State of New York.

CARLINO. You're kidding!

MIKE. Rehabilitation—it's the new thing for first offenders.

CARLINO. (*Examining the enlarger.*) What do you do? Cheese-cake? . . . Pin-ups? . . .

MIKE. And all that.

CARLINO. And all that! I always wanted to be a photographer. How much do you make?

MIKE. I do all right.

CARLINO. You always had the luck. Some jail they sent you to!

MIKE. Didn't they teach you a trade inside?

CARLINO. Oh sure . . . L and L four hours a day. (*Carlino picks Susy's apron off the top of a basket on the washing machine and holds it out for inspection.*)

MIKE. L and L . . . ?

CARLINO. Laundry and latrines . . . I'm the new Mr. Clean. (*He drapes apron around his stomach.*) Hey! You're not married, are you?

MIKE. Hell no! She just comes in to . . .

6

CARLINO. To what?

MIKE. . . . to clean up. (*Carlino lifts Susy's nightgown out of the basket.*)

CARLINO. She does more than that! (*Then he drops nightgown back and looks straight at Mike as if there is some rivalry between them.*) Lisa?

MIKE. Lisa! (*With a wry laugh.*) In a dump like this?

CARLINO. Seen her yet?

MIKE. Not a trace.

CARLINO. But you *have* looked.

MIKE. You *bet* I've looked! She owes me two grand.

CARLINO. Me too. Promised she'd double it for me by the time I got out. Instead she takes off. *I'll kill her!*

MIKE. You couldn't kill anybody. Least of all Lisa . . .

CARLINO. (*Looking around the room.*) So, where's the action?

MIKE. What action?

CARLINO. (*Impatiently.*) Like you said in your message. "If you want a quick and easy grand. . . ." So—that's what I want.

MIKE. "If you want a quick and easy grand come to 27B Grogan Street at nine exactly—door's open. . . ."

CARLINO. Only next time phone me yourself. If you'd popped out of there a second sooner you'd have caught this in your teeth. (*Shows him his brass knuckles, but Mike only looks back at him and waits for the penny to drop.*) You *did* send that message? . . . No? . . . *You* got the *same* message?

MIKE. Just like that. Then he hung up.

CARLINO. *Who* hung up?

MIKE. Search me. Thought it must be from you.

CARLINO. (*Points angrily at Sam's equipment.*) And all this? . . . Go on then—*say* it! This *isn't* your place. And you're *flat* broke! You—you're not *even* a pornographer! (*Carlino crosses to safe* D. R. *and opens front of facade.*)

MIKE. I'm worse than broke. I owe eight hundred to a loan shark and I'm a month behind with the interest.

CARLINO. (*With some relish.*) Ooo!—that's bad!

MIKE. So, if you could stake me for say—two-fifty? . . . If I don't come up with some "juice" by Monday they're taking me to the dentist.

CARLINO. Two-fifty he says! And I haven't eaten since I came

7

out. (*He picks up a camera from Sam's bench.*) How much for this?

MIKE. Cameras! You can't give 'em away. . . . So who lives here?

CARLINO. Give me a few minutes—I'll find something. (*He has just opened refrigerator.*) Now what have we here? Enough cold cuts for a long weekend— (*Opens waxed paper and takes out slices of ham, cheese, etc.*)

MIKE. Don't! (*Carlino is now looking in the freezer and discovers a twenty dollar bill at the back.*)

CARLINO. Hey! This photographer is crafty! Keeps a twenty back of the freezer!

MIKE. So leave it there. And leave that alone . . . (*Carlino stuffs the bill into his pocket and starts to search for the mustard, opening several cabinets.*) Then who does live here?

CARLINO. Now if I can just find where they hide the mustard . . .

MIKE. And who did send that message? (*As Carlino frantically searches the kitchen for mustard.*)

CARLINO. Strange how you degenerate as soon as you're free. In stir I can guzzle any slop they dish out. And now if I can't find the mustard I get the shakes!

MIKE. What did he sound like? (*Carlino has found the mustard and starts to spread it on his ham and cheese.*)

CARLINO. I got it. I got it! (*Without a care.*) What did *who* sound like?

MIKE. The joker who phoned.

CARLINO. Some kind of foreigner. Five to one it was a put-on. . . .

MIKE. Where were you when he phoned?

CARLINO. My usual place—and you?

MIKE. My usual place.

CARLINO. So?

MIKE. So?

CARLINO. (*Suddenly serious.*) Lisa?

MIKE. It's got to be Lisa. Who else knows where to find us? (*They drop their voices instinctively and are suddenly alert and tense. Carlino points to the bedroom.*)

CARLINO. What's through there? (*He runs into bedroom and out again.*)

MIKE. Bedroom and bathroom.

CARLINO. Another entrance?

MIKE. No. Bars on all the windows just like these.

CARLINO. I wonder if this place is bugged! *(Calling sharply.)* Lisa!

MIKE. Sh—Shut up!

CARLINO. *(Calling.)* Come out, come out from wherever you are! *(A long pause as though they really expected a reply. Carlino picks up his sandwich and starts to take an enormous bite when there are three knocks on the hall door. . . . They both freeze, turn to the door and then to each other.)*

MIKE. Who is it? *(No replay. Carlino suddenly panics. Mike snaps his fingers and points to the door. Carlino tiptoes upstairs and gets behind the door, putting on his knuckle-duster. Two more knocks. Carlino unlocks door. Roat opens door and peers in. He holds over one arm a dilapidated piece of carpet [about six feet long] and has an airline bag in one hand.)*

ROAT. *(To Mike politely.)* Good evening, Mr. Talman.

MIKE. You've got the wrong place . . .

ROAT. Oh, have I? . . . Then could I be interesting you in a rug for your bathroom? I'd be giving this away at six ninety-five, but for you, sir . . .

MIKE. No rugs, thank you.

ROAT. Then if I may just deliver my message . . .

MIKE. Who from?

ROAT. From the party who phoned you not half an hour ago.

MIKE. Then why the hell didn't you say so?

ROAT. Thank you, Mr. Talman.

MIKE. That's not my name. *(As Roat enters he deliberately bangs the door back against Carlino and then closes it. Carlino's hand goes to his nose. Roat speaks to Carlino without looking at him, but as if he knew he was there all the time.)*

ROAT. Oh, I beg your pardon—I had not idea you were there. *(Carlino follows Roat, dabbing his nose with his handkerchief. Roat spreads the piece of carpet D. C.)* Now I'll be candid and honest with you, gentlemen. Strictly speaking, this is not my carpet. I discovered it in a pile of junk in that torn-down building at the back of here. And seeing as it's a little damp and a bit cheesy . . . a dollar seventy-five and I'll be on my way.

CARLINO. Let's have the message—and then take that stinking thing out of here!

MIKE. Where's Lisa?

ROAT. I beg your pardon, Mr. Talman.

9

MIKE. Let's get this straight, Buster. My name is not Talman! And I've never heard of such a person.

ROAT. But it's a grand name, don't you think? *Good old Mike Talman!* . . . Don't you think it suits him fine . . . (*Turning.*) *Sergeant Carlino?*

CARLINO. Sergeant—who?

ROAT. And *you* will be Sergeant Carlino. (*A pause.*)

CARLINO. Hey, come on, who the hell are you?

ROAT. I am Harry Roat Junior *and* Senior—from Scarsdale. (*Carlino and Mike glance at each other, mystified.*)

CARLINO. Okay, Mister Roat Junior *and* Senior—the *message and out!* (*As Roat talks on he lights a cigarette from a gold case and lets the ash grow long and [later] takes from his zip-bag an empty baby food jar with a screw top which he carefully uses as an ashtray. Mike and Carlino stand listening, occasionally throwing each other a glance. Later, as they talk Roat rises and paces around, paying no attention to the other two but taking in every detail of the room. Mike and Carlino move around him like chessmen, always keeping him in between them and with one of them always blocking him from the stairs.*)

MIKE. Who sent you here?

ROAT. The message, Children, is that once upon a time there were two *small* con artists. I believe they've just come out of jail, poor fellows. (*Looking at Mike.*) One of them was tall and rugged and he'd drop in on a housewife when she was alone and pretend to be an old friend of her husband's. The other— (*Turning to Carlino.*) —would turn up a little later as a police detective. But the real brains of the outfit was a beautiful and talented girl. She could be young or old, French, Italian or Katie from Kansas . . .

MIKE. Where is Lisa?

ROAT. Both men fell for her and would make little passes when the other wasn't looking . . . (*He laughs.*) . . . and with a quite pathetic lack of success. Finally she got bored with them—made an anonymous phone call to the police and then disappeared, taking their loot with her. As they say there's no one quite so gullible as a con man in love.

CARLINO. Who sent you here? . . . And who are you? (*No reply. Amused and pleased by their curiosity, Roat simply looks from one to the other.*)

MIKE. If Lisa told you all that, why isn't she here?

CARLINO. Where is she? (*No reply.*)

MIKE. Are you working for Lisa . . . or is she working for you? (*A pause.*)

ROAT. We are now all working for Lisa. (*A pause. Carlino turns to Mike, encouraged and hopeful.*)

CARLINO. You said on the phone—a quick and easy grand.

ROAT. That is correct.

MIKE. Plus the two thousand each that Lisa already owes us.

ROAT. You shall have it.

CARLINO. When?

ROAT. Tomorrow night. *If* we succeed. If we fail—nothing.

MIKE. Why didn't Lisa come here herself?

ROAT. Perhaps she was a little shy of meeting you again *before* she could give you your money.

MIKE. So when *do* we see her?

ROAT. Tomorrow night—*with* the merchandise. . . . Well?

CARLINO. Look—we don't even talk till we get two-fifty each—

ROAT. (*Surprised.*) Lisa told me to give you *five* hundred each and the balance on delivery. Any objections? (*Carlino puts out his hand for the money.*) But first—may we have weapons on the table?

CARLINO. (*Innocently.*) Search me, I'm clean.

ROAT. Your brass-knuckles?

CARLINO. What brass-knuckles?

ROAT. In your right pocket . . . I cannot negotiate in an atmosphere of mistrust . . . (*Carlino crosses L. and drops his brass-knuckles onto table.*) And your little razor-blade, Mr. Talman. (*Mike takes out a one-edged safety razor-blade [wrapped in cardboard] and drops it on table.*)

CARLINO. And how do you protect yourself? (*From his pocket Roat takes a thin ivory statue of a girl. It is about five inches long and could be a small flashlight.*)

ROAT. Geraldine protects me. Isn't she beautiful?

CARLINO. What does she do?

ROAT. This! (*A thin switchblade springs out.*)

MIKE. (*Calmly.*) Then may we have Geraldine on the table too?

ROAT. We may not. (*The blade disappears and Roat returns knife to his pocket and also the razor blade and knuckle duster.*)

CARLINO. Why the hell not?

ROAT. Because she is the referee. (*Roat hands them each a wad of*

11

money. *Carlino counts his greedily and examines each note at kitchen worklight, but Mike, playing hard to get, tosses his back onto the table.*)

MIKE. Not yet, Mr. Roat . . . what's the merchandise?

ROAT. A child's doll.

MIKE. A doll?

ROAT. A musical doll. Lisa last saw it a few days ago in Montreal. (*A pause, then slowly.*) But she now believes it is *somewhere* in *this* apartment.

MIKE. How did it get *here*?

ROAT. While Lisa was at the airport in Montreal she got into conversation with a very nice photographer named Sam Hendrix and she asked him if he would take this doll to her little girl who was in the New York Hospital. And he was most sympathetic. But before he had time to deliver it, Lisa arrived at this apartment herself and asked for it. And then, much to her surprise—he just couldn't find it. (*Mike picks up his roll of bills from table and pockets them.*)

CARLINO. What do you mean—he couldn't find it?

ROAT. He couldn't find it. Lisa watched him search both these rooms and finally—pretending it was of no importance—she left. That was last night.

MIKE. How big is this doll? (*Roat measures twenty inches. Mike says impatiently.*) Weight?

ROAT. Just under two pounds.

MIKE. (*To Carlino.*) Allow eight ounces for the music box . . !

CARLINO. That's a lot of *"horse!"*

MIKE. (*To Roat.*) Is this the real stuff . . . *pure* heroin?

ROAT. Nothing has ever been so pure.

CARLINO. That'll be worth over fifty grand. Do you push it yourself?

ROAT. Now Children! . . . Let's not get too greedy—let's find the doll first, shall we?

MIKE. So Lisa sent *you* here to find it. Why does she need us?

ROAT. This morning Lisa phoned this number . . . (*Points to phone.*) and pretending she was an Italian actress named Liciana, she made an appointment to have some portraits taken by Mr. Hendrix at his studio tonight. Mr. and Mrs. Hendrix left this house just before seven. They walked to a movie where he left his wife and then he went on to his studio where he is still waiting . . .

12

CARLINO. (Interrupting.) Now hold it! (To Mike.) Are you getting any of this?

MIKE. (Impatiently.) Sure. Just pay attention.

CARLINO. Well, I'm lost!

MIKE. So listen!

CARLINO. Look—Mr. Roat. I'm a first grade drop-out. Just give it to me like A-B-C . . . Lisa wants to get them out of here so she can come in and really go through this place. Right?

ROAT. (Picks up phone and starts to dial.) That is correct.

CARLINO. So right now the wife is watching a movie and the photographer is at his studio waiting for some Italian broad who doesn't even exist. How long is he going to wait?

ROAT. Perhaps we had better reassure him . . . if you'll excuse me . . . (Into phone.) . . . hello? Mr. Sam Hendrix? . . . Ah, I am so glad! I am Giano of Giano's restaurant. I have a message from Miss Liciana. She is so very sorry to be late . . . no, wait, please. She is on her way to you now. I put her in a taxi two minutes ago . . . (In Italian, very fast.) Il taxi per La Signorina Liciana subito . . . (In English.) Mr. Hendrix? . . . Any minute Miss Liciana will arrive. Be kind and wait for her? . . . Thank you, sir. Goodbye. (Roat hangs up phone.) That should hold him there a bit longer.

MIKE. So Lisa has been in here already tonight?

ROAT. Yes. And she searched everywhere and still couldn't find it.

CARLINO. So she searched everywhere? How did she open this? (Carlino hits filing cabinet and rattles handle.)

MIKE. And there's a closet in the bedroom that's locked too. I'll open that right now. (Mike starts towards bedroom.)

ROAT. It's not in the closet.

MIKE. How do you know?

ROAT. Lisa looked. She found the key on the ledge just above it.

CARLINO. (Throwing back facade to reveal safe [i.e. to audience].) And this? (As Mike goes to safe and examines it.)

MIKE. (To Roat.) Well? Does Lisa know about this safe?

ROAT. She does . . . and that's why you're here.

CARLINO. (After a visual consultation with Mike.) Well—this is a bit out of our line but—okay, we'll make the photographer open it when he gets back here. . . . But look— (With a grim laugh.) we aren't squeamish, Mr. Roat . . . are you?

ROAT. I am. And that is not why you're here. Suppose—after

some persuasion—he *did* unlock the safe and it *wasn't* there? Then what?

CARLINO. The doll's in that safe—give you five to one.

ROAT. That's a chance Lisa won't take. (*Pointing at safe.*) It *may* be in there. Or he may have taken it somewhere else. He may *even* have given it to the police. We have to slide into this very gently. Believe me—Lisa didn't call you two in for nothing—

MIKE. (*Impatiently.*) What did she say?

ROAT. She said—"Don't let them twist any arms and you're not to steal anything . . . let the *wife* find the doll—and give it to *you* . . . (*Points at Mike.*) . . . of her own free will." (*Carlino appears delighted and smacks Mike on the back.*)

CARLINO. Well—this is like old times. So we con 'em out of it! (*To Mike.*) You betta find out all you can about this guy. (*As if this is all a matter of fixed routine, Mike and Carlino go into action. While Carlino jumps onto stool and peeps through Venetian blinds, Mike empties the whole of the garbage pail onto floor [or bench] and goes through its contents [i.e. crumpled envelopes, Sam's used airline ticket, etc.]. Roat stands quietly and watches them with interest. Carlino, to Roat:*) What's his name again?

MIKE. (*Reading off airline ticket.*) Hendrix—Sam Hendrix . . . flew to Montreal . . . last Monday returned New York . . . yesterday.

CARLINO. (*Looking through blinds.*) Hey! And look what I can see—right by the parking lot!

MIKE. What?

CARLINO. A phone booth!

MIKE. Great! And *two* blinds. Which gives us *nine* signals. (*Mike and Carlino argue terribly fast. We do not need to follow them.*)

CARLINO. Six.

MIKE. Nine.

CARLINO. Up—open and down. Three two's are six.

MIKE. It's three *squared*, you fink!

ROAT. Now you've left me behind.

CARLINO. Just a little system of ours. One of us goes zonk-zonk . . . (*He flips the blinds open and shut quickly and then jumps off stool and picks up phone.*) And then the phone rings. (*He hangs up phone.*) Just leave this to us, Mr. Roat.

ROAT. Thank you. (*A pause during which he takes out two small notebooks.*) Oh by the way—the *number* of that phone booth in the parking lot is 924-5309. (*Mike and Carlino glance at each other in amazement. Roat copies the phone number [which is already in one of the notebooks] into the other one and hands them a notebook each.*) Here. (*Still bewildered they take them. Roat then points to phone on table.*) Now make a note of this number. (*As they each write it down, Roat points to photograph [of Marines] above Sam's bench.*) And there's some information on that wall, Mike. (*As Mike goes to Marine picture and makes note.*)

CARLINO. (*To Roat.*) When do we start all this? Tonight?

ROAT. Tomorrow. A proud grandfather from Asbury Park will phone Mr. Hendrix and ask him to come there and take some pictures of his family *tomorrow afternoon* . . . one hour by express bus—seventy-five dollars and stay to dinner. And that gets the husband out of the way. (*During above speech—Mike has slipped into bedroom. Roat now realizes he has left the room.*) There's a Volkswagen bus . . . Mike? (*Mike enters.*) Oh, there you are. There's a Volkswagen bus out there in the car lot. (*Pointing towards windows.*) I'll meet you there in ten minutes. (*Carlino starts to go upstairs. Roat packs things into zip bag, collects coat, etc.*)

MIKE. You staying here—Mr. Roat?

ROAT. (*Casually.*) Just a quick look around—in case I've forgotten anything.

MIKE. We'll stay with you then.

ROAT. Better not all leave together.

MIKE. I guess you're right. (*To Carlino.*) Come on, then, Sergeant Carlino. (*Then turns back to Roat.*) Oh, by the way—the key of that bedroom closet. (*A pause.*)

ROAT. What about it?

MIKE. It's *not* on the ledge.

ROAT. Isn't it? Then Lisa must have taken it with her. (*Mike is now watching Roat very carefully. Carlino has reached the hall door but turns. Mike moves close to camera tripod.*)

MIKE. Won't they miss it? . . . When they get back tonight?

ROAT. (*With a shrug.*) They'll each think the other one lost it.

MIKE. Then there's just one question—before we leave here.

ROAT. Yes?

MIKE. Lisa told you an awful lot, didn't she.

ROAT. Lisa?

MIKE. Lisa. All those little details about how she worked . . .

CARLINO. And about us.

MIKE. You see, we know Lisa very well . . .

CARLINO. Yeah, and she would never give you anything . . .

MIKE. Unless she had to.

ROAT. So? . . . What's your question?

MIKE. We'd just like to know where you've hidden the key of that locked closet in there. (*Roat whips out his zip knife and takes a step towards Carlino.*)

ROAT. All right, you—through that door backwards and turn that way. (*Carlino backs up the stairs.*)

MIKE. Catch! (*Mike picks up the spiked camera tripod and tosses it to Carlino. At the same time Mike picks up the kitchen chair and holds it like a lion tamer. All this in a very few seconds. Then they all stand motionless, Roat's eyes moving from one to the other. Mike, quietly:*) Now, drop "Geraldine" on the floor—nice and easy.

ROAT. I'd rather not do that . . .

MIKE. Drop it! (*The two men move in suddenly.*)

ROAT. Children ! . . Children ! . . (*They stop.*) Will you settle for this? (*Roat pockets knife and holds up key.*)

MIKE. Flip it! (*Roat tosses key to Mike. Mike catches it and puts down the chair [between settee and Sam's bench] and with a glance to Carlino crosses to bedroom door. Just before exiting to bedroom, he says:*) Why don't you sit down, Mr. Roat?

ROAT. Thank you. (*But doesn't move. Carlino holds out the tripod like a three-pronged bayonet and advances slowly on Roat.*)

CARLINO. Now! (*Roat crosses to settee and sits facing bedroom door. Mike goes into the bedroom. We hear him unlock and open the closet door. [Pause.] A bed lamp is switched on for five seconds and then off. [Pause.] Mike enters from bedroom. He is obviously shocked by what he has seen.*)

MIKE. (*Quietly.*) You dirty little creep! (*He takes out his wad of notes, drops them on the floor and starts to go. To Carlino.*) Come on. (*But Carlino is too curious and he hands the tripod to Mike and goes into the bedroom himself.*) Don't! (*While Carlino is in there Mike looks at Roat. Roat looks straight back at him like an innocent schoolboy wrongly accused of cheating at math. The lamp goes on and off in bedroom but quicker this time.*) Why?

ROAT. (*Sadly.*) Lisa was too clever, Mike. I felt certain she knew where it was—and then—too late. (*Carlino enters from bedroom,*) slamming the door. *He is in a panic. He throws his money onto the floor and almost runs up the stairs. Mike has placed the tripod back where he found it. Just as they are about to exit, Roat says, very calmly:*) You've—forgotten something . . . (*Only Carlino turns.*)

MIKE. Come on!

ROAT. You're already involved—aren't you? (*Carlino takes step down.*)

CARLINO. (*In a thick voice.*) I can prove where I was when this happened.

ROAT. Oh? Exactly when did it happen? (*Pause.*) Just before you let me in? By the way I am not on parole and no policeman has ever heard of me.

CARLINO. But someone must have seen you with her *somewhere* . . .

ROAT. Never. I've *followed* her several times but we never actually met until she walked in there tonight.

CARLINO. All that stuff about us . . . she told you all that tonight?

ROAT. That and a good deal more.

MIKE. You just try and get away with this—but—we—are—out! You're on your own now, Mr. Roat! (*To Carlino.*) Come on.

ROAT. Sorry, Mike—but you were both so highly recommended. I need you.

CARLINO. Well, that's just too bad!—And now you've got a body in there and *you* are *stuck* with it. (*Opens door and starts to exit. To Mike:*) Let's go.

ROAT. Now just listen, Children . . . think, think, think. If you walk out on me now, I will simply walk out after you and leave Lisa in there. You've signed your names all over this apartment . . . (*Carlino comes downstairs and starts to go around the room, almost pathetically, rubbing his fingerprints off everything he can remember touching—his only problem: he can't remember.*) And even if you could remember what you've touched it would take at least an hour to wipe off. (*He takes out a pair of loose plastic gloves and puts them on and then wipes telephone.*) Now I have touched only one thing since you came in here and before that I wore *these.* Highly recommended, by the way—and disposable— you buy them in *enormous* rolls from Hammacher Schlemmer. Don't forget the safe, Sergeant . . . and the icebox. (*Carlino is*

17

frantic on his double-take from safe to icebox. Roat watches him a moment with interest and amusement.) Now just do exactly what I tell you and the police will never even come in here. *(Impatiently to Carlino.)* Will you stop acting like a housemaid and listen! You've got all tomorrow to do that. Now, *one*—get her out of here. Roll her up in this— *(He kicks old carpet.)* and dump it where I found it, and then meet me in the Volkswagen. *(Carlino, in a fit of frustration and confusion, throws down his wiping cloth.)*

CARLINO. *(Pleading.)* Look—just let us out of this? *(Turns to Mike for help.)*

ROAT. No. I need you.

MIKE. *(Desperately.)* For what?

ROAT. *(As though to calm them down.)* Everything we just planned still holds good . . . we simply con the wife until she finds us that doll and that's it. No one gets hurt—not even a scratch. *(Mike and Carlino are now standing still and listening to him like schoolboys.)* There is just one minor difference, perhaps. That instead of working for Lisa—you are now working for me.

MIKE. *(Picking up his money.)* Then there's one other difference, Mr. Roat. You promised us our two thousand plus one each?

ROAT. Less this five hundred, of course.

MIKE. *(Pointing at bedroom.)* But things have changed since then.

CARLINO. *(Picking up his money.)* Yeah.

ROAT. All right . . . two plus two—then.

MIKE. We want two thousand plus another *five* thousand *each*—tomorrow night. *(Street door slams, off U. L.)*

ROAT. Quiet! *(They listen. We can hear Susy's blind stick in hall. Roat gestures Mike and Carlino to take up their positions—Mike has run upstairs and stands behind door. Roat points at carpet. Carlino picks it up and goes D. R. and switches off room lights [but has not time to switch off bedroom light]. Roat moves D. L., [because it is in his way, he picks up garbage pail and puts it on top of washer]. The room is lit dimly by light from bedroom [door open]. Roat, in a whisper:)* She's alone . . . stay exactly where you are and don't even breathe. *(They all freeze. Sound of key in door and Susy enters. She wears a raincoat and a purse bag is slung from her shoulder. She should move quietly and easily as though she knows this apartment well. She hangs stick and bag on railing.)*

SUSY. Sammy! *(As she exits to bedroom, she feels the position of* light switch [i.e. off].) Sam? (*She enters from bedroom, takes a few steps into room and then stops and listens.*) Gloria? (*She crosses to clock D. L., feels it and then dials on phone.*) Sam . . . (*Quietly, almost in whisper.*) well—what does she look like—*The Liciana!* . . . (*Loudly.*) You mean she hasn't even arrived yet? . . . *Delayed?* For nearly two hours? Who does she think you are? . . . I'm home *now* . . . oh—the movie was great—but you should have checked, honey . . . it was in Swedish! (*Makes Swedish noises.*) And not even a note of background music. (*Pause, listens.*) Well—I *tried* to walk home but I took a wrong turn somewhere so I came by taxi, how else? . . . *Yes, a taxi!* . . . (*A pause.*) You mean—walk to your studio *now?* Oh no—I'm staying right here. When will you be home? (*A pause, she listens.*) Eleven! . . . well, in *that* case I'd better trot over right now and keep the score . . . oh you needn't worry, I won't cramp your style . . . ciaou! (*She hangs up. She goes to stairs, but on her way she knocks into the small chair which Mike left below Sam's bench. Gently.*) Ooo!—you little . . . (*She feels around for the table, lifts chair, and then plonks it down fiercely in its proper place.*) *You* . . . are supposed to be—*there!* (*She starts towards the stairs and then stops suddenly.*) Gloria! (*A pause. Then she speaks exactly as though she was talking to the three men.*) O come on . . . I *know* you're there . . . you can't fool me, you know. (*A pause—while she listens—then realizing she is wrong she moves on. Mike spreads himself out against the wall as she goes up the stairs. She picks up her stick and exits, slamming the door. We hear her stick trailing along the other side of the back wall, and the front door opens and slams.*)

CARLINO. (*Drops carpet.*) Phew!

ROAT. (*To Mike.*) Well?

MIKE. (*Without moving.*) Two plus five, Mr. Roat?

ROAT. (*With a polite little bow.*) Two plus five, Mr. Talman. (*Mike comes down stairs, turns to Carlino and jerks his head toward the bedroom. Then each picking up one end of the carpet, they carry it into the bedroom. Roat does not help them but stands calmly and watches them exit.*)

CURTAIN

END OF ACT I, SCENE 1

ACT I

SCENE 2

TIME: *Saturday afternoon (about 4:15 p.m.).*

ON RISE: *Though it is still light outside the stage is completely blacked-out for Sam is now using the room as his photographic darkroom, i.e. the black-out arrangement is over both windows, both doors are closed, lights off in hall and bedroom (drapes closed in bedroom), etc. So we can see nothing. For several seconds we only hear Sam and Susy. He is working at his bench and she is moving, easily, between table and sink (rattle plates, silver, etc.) as she clears the table.*

NOTE: *Most of Sam's photo equipment is packed up at foot of stairs, ready to go.*

After a few seconds, Susy speaks:

SUSY. Hear about the murder?

SAM. Just two seconds . . . (*A pause, then light in Sam's enlarger goes on for exactly two seconds.*) . . . what murder?

SUSY. They found a body this morning—somewhere near *here.*

SAM. Who told you?

SUSY. On the radio. I only heard the end of it. A woman from Scarsdale—or somewhere.

SAM. You making this up?

SUSY. Why should I? (*Sam switches on amber safe light and lamp on bench [at lamp itself].*)

SAM. It's a ploy to make me stay home.

SUSY. It is not.

SAM. Okay windows. (*As they talk Sam develops the enlargement and Susy moves around the room undoing the black-out [it is dull and rainy outside], then crosses to bedroom door to switch on the room lights. [See later.]* You'd rather I didn't go?

SUSY. Serious.

SAM. Of course.

SUSY. Well, no. I mean *yes* I always want you to stay home. But not because somebody's been murdered . . . because of me. Need the ceiling lights?

SAM. Yes please, it's a bit gloomy. (*By bedroom door, Susy*

20

switches on ceiling lights and also switches off Sam's bench lamp.)
That one I need.
SUSY. Sorry. *(She switches on his bench lamp from door.)*
SAM. Now—quick check. Phone number for Police Emergency?
SUSY. Oh—just dial zero and say you're blind.
SAM. Operators get busy and don't answer.
SUSY. Oh! That urgent! So that murder *does* worry you.
SAM. This one you *must* know. Four four zero . . . one two
three four. *(As Susy gets sugar lumps, takes out four and lays
them in a row by phone.)*
SUSY. Wait till I get the sugar lumps. Four four owe . . . one
two three four. It's these easy ones that fool me . . . so it's *four*—
not four owe four *not* owe four four but *four four owe* one two
three four?
SAM. Then ask for the Sixth Precinct. *(Sam has hung up his enlargement to dry and now starts to finish packing his photo equip-
ment and preparing to leave.)*
SUSY. Sixth Precinct. Four plus two, okay. *(Rapidly.)* Doctor's
office 924-6381. Want the Chinese laundry?
SAM. Now—my bus leaves at five and they return from . . .
where?
SUSY. Asbury Park.
SAM. At . . . ?
SUSY. Er . . . every hour on the hour.
SAM. *(Rapidly.)* I'll phone you as soon as I get there and again
when I'm leaving. Oh—and if that doll woman phones just say I
still haven't found it.
SUSY. Okay.
SAM. And try and get her phone number.
SUSY. Maybe Gloria's seen the doll.
SAM. No she hasn't. I asked her mother. But let Gloria look
around for it while she's down here. It must be *somewhere.*
SUSY. That child isn't coming here today.
SAM. Just to do your shopping. Grocery list and five dollars by
the phone.
SUSY. *No Gloria!* *(Susy knocks a pepper shaker [or something]
onto the floor with an impatient wave of her hand. She waits as
though hoping that Sam will pick it up—but he doesn't.)* Okay
then where is it?
SAM. Not listening?

SUSY. Not listening!

SAM. Near the table (*or wherever*). (*Susy gets down and feels around for it with her hand.*) What's wrong with Gloria?

SUSY. Everything. She can't even close the icebox. Am I anywhere *near*?

SAM. Yes—but you're not searching. . . . Try twenty degrees left (*or whatever*). If she doesn't close the icebox—just say— "close the icebox." (*Susy's hand searches around in a wider circle till she finds it.*)

SUSY. And if she still doesn't?

SAM. Then just say "that's the girl—*thanks.*"

SUSY. What do you mean—that's the girl—*thanks?* It's *still open.*

SAM. A little trick I learnt in the Marines, sweetheart—always *assume* that an order's been carried out. Then if she hasn't closed it already she'll be so *embarrassed* . . .

SUSY. Gloria isn't a Marine—she doesn't embarrass that easily . . . I'd much rather have a dog. (*Susy gets up from the floor, returns pepper shaker and, later, searches for garbage pail under sink.*)

SAM. Dogs can't shop at the supermarket.

SUSY. Dogs can't rearrange the furniture. That's Gloria's latest hobby. Whenever we're out she borrows her mother's key and sneaks in here and turns everything around. I nearly broke both my legs last night. Now *where* has she hidden the garbage pail? I've been hunting for it all morning. (*Sam takes it off washer [where Roat left it last night] and hands it to Susy.*)

SAM. Here . . . now you put it back where it belongs.

SUSY. Where was it?

SAM. On top of the washer. Where *you* must have put it.

SUSY. (*Returning garbage pail to closet under sink.*) It was Gloria!

SAM. (*Putting on his raincoat.*) Oh come on now—take it easy on this kid. Her daddy's just left them again. And her mother's out looking for *him.* She's been battered back and forth like a sawed-off shuttlecock. And on top of that she's having to wear glasses for the first time. By the way—call her Four-Eyes. (*Sam lights cigarette.*)

SUSY. Four-Eyes!

SAM. The glasses. That's what the kids are calling her and she can't take it so they'll go on till she can.

SUSY. So?

SAM. So if *we* call her that too—she'll get used to it much quicker.

SUSY. I don't know if I dare. (*Sam takes power-pack out of icebox and then packs it with his photo-kit.*)

SAM. Now you're scared of a nine-year-old girl. The icebox needs defrosting. But *my* way this time.

SUSY. *Your* way! And if I burn both my hands off?

SAM. Don't. *Unguentine's* in the emergency drawer.

SUSY. Defrost the icebox! Do I have to have a project *every* time you're away?

SAM. And if it stops raining—try walking over to my studio and back. And no cheating.

SUSY. Did I cheat last night?

SAM. How about that old lady who helped you across Sixth Avenue?

SUSY. You were *watching*?!

SAM. Only while you crossed Sixth. How about it, huh? Just once to the studio and back? All by yourself. (*Sam puts his cigarette in ash tray on top of safe. Buttons up his raincoat, buckles belt, etc.*)

SUSY. *Do I have to be the world's champion blind woman?*

SAM. *Yes!*

SUSY. How about just a little old bronze medal now and then? *I'm an awfully good loser?*

SAM. Much sooner have a winner. (*He holds out his hand.*) I'm holding out for you, sweetheart. (*Susy crosses to Sam and feels around for his hand but he keeps moving it around so she can not find it [a love game]. Finally she grabs it and laughs.*)

SUSY. Hey! You cheat! I've been there once already. (*They hug and kiss.*) Just don't *ever* leave me.

SAM. Fat chance! (*Susy moves back a pace away from Sam.*)

SUSY. Is she waiting for you at the bus station?

SAM. It's a *he*—I'm meeting him at . . .

SUSY. No—I mean the woman who didn't turn up last night— *Liciana!*

SAM. Oh *her*. Yes. She went on ahead to get the back seat. (*Susy takes two wild swipes at his face with u. hand but misses. Sam laughs.*) Nowhere near! (*Sam leans down to pick up a piece of his equipment [or bag] and as he rises Susy swipes with d. hand and hits him. He lets out a cry.*)

SUSY. Gosh I'm sorry, honey. I didn't know you were *there!*

SAM. I'm *here!* Now take it easy.

SUSY. But admit it that's my first lucky punch in weeks.

SAM. Yes—you were lucky and I've got a nose bleed and I'm going to miss that bus. (*He goes up the stairs with all his bags and equipment, opens door.*)

SUSY. Oh—just tell me one thing. Where does the icebox plug in?

SAM. Huh?

SUSY. The refrigerator . . . where does it plug into the wall?

SAM. Oh—you'll find it . . . and don't ask Gloria either.

SUSY. I don't need Gloria . . . and I certainly don't need you.

SAM. Hah! (*Sam closes door and exits L. A few seconds later we see him walk past the windows outside. Left to herself Susy appears a little depressed at the prospect of a lonely uneventful day ahead of her. She wonders what to do next then disappears into the bedroom and several seconds later enters carrying an armful of laundry. While she is in bedroom the ashtray on top of safe [where Sam left his lighted cigarette] begins to smoke. Susy takes several paces towards the washer before she notices the smell. Then turns and sniffs around trying to locate the direction from which the smoke is coming.*)

SUSY. (*Calling.*) Sam! . . . Gloria! . . . Anybody! (*Then she panics and runs up the stairs but stumbles, drops laundry on stairs, then gets hold of herself and turns back, crosses to phone and dials zero. During the above we see Mike cross window outside on his way to street door. Susy, into phone:*) Fire Department please— (*A long pause.*) Oh hello! . . . Fire Department? . . . I hate to bother you about a little thing like this but—hello . . . I think there's something burning . . . it may only be a cigarette—but I'm blind and I can't seem to locate it and it's getting worse! Could you send someone over, or would it be quicker if I phoned the police do you think? . . . Yes, of course, I'm sorry, it's 27B— (*The hall doorbell rings.*) Just a second—I think someone's here. (*She lays phone on table, i.e. does not hang up.*) Come in, come in, whoever you are! (*She runs up the stairs. Mike opens the door and enters. He is now dressed like a junior executive. He wears a raincoat which he later takes off.*)

MIKE. Mrs. Hendrix?

SUSY. Oh, good!

MIKE. My name's Tal . . .

SUSY. (*Quickly.*) Oh, that's all right, come in! I think there's something on fire. Can you . . . ?

MIKE. Look out! (*In coming down the stairs too fast Susy trips over laundry and Mike grabs her just in time. He holds her for a few seconds until she recovers her balance.*) Easy now . . . O.K.?

SUSY. Can you see it anywhere? I'm blind, you see.

MIKE. (*Calmly.*) I got it. (*Note: when Mike caught Susy on the stairs he dropped a package which he was carrying. He now picks it up and when he takes the ashtray off the top of the safe he leaves package in its place [on purpose]. He then takes ashtray to sink and puts out the burning butt.*) It was only a cigarette butt. There was a little paper in the ashtray. Must have caught fire.

SUSY. Oh, thank you. Where *was* the ash tray?

MIKE. On the say . . . (*He stops just in time. He was going to say "safe."*) . . . by the wall mirror.

SUSY. Silly of me. I can never *quite* tell where smoke's coming from. I don't know you, do I?

MIKE. No, Mrs. Hendrix. My name's Talman. Mike Talman. I used to know Sam.

SUSY. Oh! I'm Susy Hendrix. (*She puts out her hand and they shake.*) But I'm afraid you've just missed him—he won't be back 'til tonight.

MIKE. Oh, that's too bad. I'm flying to Phoenix in a couple of hours.

SUSY. I'm sorry.

MIKE. I should have phoned, of course. I did try last night . . . about nine o'clock but . . . (*Mike picks up laundry from stairs.*)

SUSY. Yes, we were out. Do you often come to New York? (*Mike puts laundry into her hand.*)

MIKE. Here's your laundry.

SUSY. Oh, thank you.

MIKE. No—some friends lent me their apartment for a few days—it's quite near here. I thought I saw Sam last night on Eighth Street. I was passing in a cab—so I looked him up in the phone book. (*Susy puts laundry in washer.*)

SUSY. Yes, he has a studio near there. Sit down, won't you? (*Waving toward settee.*)

MIKE. (*Hesitating.*) Well, just for a minute, thank you. (*Looking around the room.*) I see he's still a camera bug.

SUSY. Yes, he began studying when he left the Marines . . . was that where you . . . ?

MIKE. Yes, it was. (*Realizing he is late on cue, Mike quickly takes out the small drugstore notebook [which Roat gave him last night] and turns the pages, searching.*)

SUSY. You were in the . . . ? (*As he can't find it Mike peers round at the photograph on the wall and half rises but it is just too far away—so he returns to his notebook and turns page.*)

MIKE. The . . . seems so long ago I've almost forgotten . . . the . . . *I got it!* . . .

SUSY. No, don't tell me the—the third training battalion—*Charlie Company!*

MIKE. (*Together, from notebook.*) Charlie Company! That's it! (*With a laugh.*) Good old Charlie Company! (*Surprised.*) Did you know Sam in those days?

SUSY. Oh no—we first met about a year ago—just after my accident—and got married six months later. (*Mike makes a note in notebook.*)

MIKE. You lost your sight in an accident?

SUSY. (*Quite cheerfully.*) Yes—an automobile accident.

MIKE. Sam and I first met five feet under water—but I guess he's told you that one.

SUSY. No.

MIKE. I drove my Jeep into a canal. In fact—I guess he saved my life.

SUSY. Well that makes two of us!

MIKE. Oh? (*Susy sits near Mike.*)

SUSY. I was practicing how to cross at the lights and cars were piling up all round me by the time Sam yanked me out and he wasn't very polite about it, either!

MIKE. Oh Boy! You don't have to tell me!

SUSY. Were you scared of him?

MIKE. We all were—till we got to know him, of course. He was just a perfectionist I guess.

SUSY. And he still is! Of course *he's* the one who should be blind. He'd be terribly good at it. (*Mike begins to laugh as if he cannot help it.*)

MIKE. Blind Sam! . . . (*Laughs.*) I know I shouldn't laugh, Mrs. Hendrix, but—

SUSY. (*Highly amused.*) Oh that's all right! Now he *would* be the world's champion blind man . . . (*They both laugh together. As Susy is speaking the door opens quietly and Gloria looks in and watches them for a moment. Susy, calling:*) Gloria? (*To Mike.*) Who is that?

MIKE. A little girl. (*Mike rises, after glancing at Gloria he turns away so as not to be recognized.*)

SUSY. (*Louder.*) Come in, Gloria!

MIKE. (*After a pause.*) She went out . . . does Sam . . . does Sam still get up to Canada now and then?

SUSY. Yes he was visiting his parents there last week . . . did you ever meet them? (*Mike makes note: "visiting parents."*)

MIKE. Er—no, I never did. Well I'm sure sorry to have missed him, Mrs. . . . (*He goes upstairs.*)

SUSY. Drop us a card next time you're around. (*Susy rises and goes to below landing.*)

MIKE. Thank you, Mrs. Hendrix.

SUSY. Susy.

MIKE. Susy. Well, I better go pick up my bags. Just say hello to Sam for me.

SUSY. (*Trying to remember his name.*) Uhhh?

MIKE. Mike Talman.

SUSY. Mike Talman.

MIKE. That's right. (*Susy puts out her hand and they shake again over the railing.*)

SUSY. Well goodbye . . . and thanks for putting out the . . . oh, my God! (*Susy hurries to phone and grabs it off table. While she is talking on phone Mike opens door. Gloria is standing outside. He exits L. and Gloria enters quietly and stands at the top of the stairs watching Susy, who does not notice her. Gloria is nine years old and wears glasses. Susy, into phone:*) Hello . . . oh—you're still there. I'm terribly sorry but the fire's out. As a matter of fact it wasn't in here at all. It was upstairs—just some soup that had burnt up on the stove but you could smell it for blocks! . . . Yes, you see there was a little girl up there and she was supposed to be watching it, but you know how they are sometimes—oh, no, she's fine and so it's all out now. Goodbye. (*Hangs up.*) Oh—how awful! Mike? . . . Mike?

GLORIA. *What* soup?

SUSY. Oh—hello, Gloria.

GLORIA. (*Quietly, coming down stairs.*) Who was that man who was in here?

SUSY. That was Mr. Talman . . . he's an old friend of Sam's.

GLORIA. Oh, I see. Is the grocery list ready?

SUSY. Yes. It's by the phone. And five dollars . . . can you see it?

GLORIA. (*Picking them up.*) Yes, I have it. What else?

SUSY. Nothing else . . . (*Cheerfully.*) my job for today is to defrost the icebox . . . if you'd like to help me. (*Wasting no time, Gloria goes straight to the refrigerator, switches it to defrost and, leaving refrigerator door open, starts towards stairs.*) What did you do then?

GLORIA. Switched it to defrost, of course.

SUSY. No—that's not how *we* do it.

GLORIA. It is too. I've done it for Mother—hundreds of times.

SUSY. Not with this one. If you switch *this* one to defrost the milk freezes solid and all the jars crack open. We have to do it Sam's way. We just pull out the cord at the back and take *everything* out and put two pans of boiling water into the freezer.

GLORIA. (*Overlapping.*) Okay, do it Sam's way then. I'll go to the A & P . . . (*As Gloria reaches stairs.*)

SUSY. Did you close the door . . . of the icebox? (*Gloria glances from the open refrigerator to Susy and back.*)

GLORIA. Yes.

SUSY. I didn't hear it shut.

GLORIA. Okay, then, it's open.

SUSY. (*Calmly.*) Then will you shut it, please.

GLORIA. Can't you shut it yourself? It's right by you. (*Susy pretends to be busy at sink—hums to herself.*)

SUSY. That's the girl . . . thanks.

GLORIA. For what?

SUSY. (*Surprised.*) Oh! I thought you closed it!

GLORIA. Well I didn't.

SUSY. (*Letting go.*) Now look here, Four-Eyes! I thought I'd made this clear. When I open the icebox I close it and when you open . . . (*At the name "Four-Eyes," Gloria goes into a controlled rage. She knocks an ashtray off side table and then stands facing Susy, waiting for a fight. Susy, quietly:*) Did you drop that by mistake?

GLORIA. No.

28

SUSY. Then pick it up . . . *now!* (*Gloria goes to table, picks up jar, but seeing it is breakable puts it back and throws knives and , spoons, etc. onto floor instead.*)

GLORIA. (*Through her teeth.*) Don't you ever call me that again. (*Loudly.*) AND I DO NOT STEAL?

SUSY. Steal? Who said anything about stealing?

GLORIA. (*Loudly.*) *You* did! I know *Sam* wouldn't say a thing like that. You told Mother I'd stolen a *doll* of yours. What would I want with a silly doll?

SUSY. I never said anything of the kind. And whatever you threw down then—pick it up! (*Shouting.*) At *once!* (*Gloria now goes right round the sink and closets, systematically dropping everything she can see [which will not break or damage] onto the floor. As she does this, she shouts angrily:*)

GLORIA. And don't you shout at me! . . . I—don't—like—being —shouted—at! *Understand?* (*Susy puts her hands to her ears and shouts.*)

SUSY. You stop that—whatever you're doing—stop it! You little . . . *sawed-off shuttlecock!* (*Gloria stops dropping things and stares at Susy, a coffee pot still in her hands.*)

GLORIA. (*Quietly.*) *What* did you say?

SUSY. (*Quietly, ashamed of herself.*) I'm sorry, Gloria, I—I shouldn't have said that. (*Gloria lays down coffee pot.*)

GLORIA. What does it *mean?*

SUSY. Nothing. It just popped out—see what happens when you push someone too far? . . . (*Gloria moves towards Susy.*)

GLORIA. I know some dirty words *too*, you know . . .

SUSY. . . . And I wouldn't have called you Four-Eyes either if . . .

GLORIA. So why *did* you?

SUSY. Doesn't Sam call you that?

GLORIA. Sam *likes* me. He can call me what he likes.

SUSY. Oh, I see, thanks. I'll tell him.

GLORIA. *What* will you tell him? (*No reply, then slowly.*) If you tell Sam *anything* about this—I'll tell *him!*

SUSY. What?

GLORIA. (*Slowly.*) About that *man*—who was here just now!—*I heard!*

SUSY. What do you mean—*I heard?* (*Gloria notices Mike's package on the safe. She picks it up and reads:*)

GLORIA. From M. Tal-man . . . Ari-zona! . . . Well!

SUSY. What have you got there?

GLORIA. He left a package on the safe. By mistake I'm *sure*.

SUSY. You better leave it there.

GLORIA. Of course . . . *he'll* be back.

SUSY. I don't like you today—I think you better go.

GLORIA. Okay. I'll go then. (*She crosses to refrigerator and slams door hard.*) I've *closed* the icebox.

SUSY. And leave the grocery list—*and* the money. I'll do it myself. (*Gloria plonks list and money on settee table and goes upstairs. Susy suddenly remembers the things on the floor.*) Oh . . . but before you go, pick those things up . . . all of them . . . go on . . . put each one back where it came from. If you can't remember where—give it to me.

GLORIA. (*Hesitates.*) Will you tell Sam?

SUSY I tell Sam *everything*.

GLORIA. (*Quietly.*) Then pick them up yourself. (*Once again Susy is about to explode, but instead she becomes very controlled.*)

SUSY. (*Very quietly.*) O.K. . . . I will. (*Susy gets down slowly on her knees and feels around, gathering all she can find into one pile on the floor. Gloria stands at top of stairs and watches.*) Now beat it! Go on—get out of here . . . and don't ever come down here again. (*Susy goes on collecting on the floor and Gloria watches. She notices how Susy keeps missing things by inches. Gloria begins to wish all this had never happened. Maybe she'll lose Sam as well. Then she comes down the stairs.*)

GLORIA. (*Quietly.*) Please don't tell Sam. (*Pause.*) Susy . . . ? (*No reply.*) I wanted to help you today. (*No reply. Susy goes on trying to pick up. Gloria picks up something that Susy has missed twice and puts it into Susy's hand.*)

SUSY. (*Quietly.*) Thanks. I'll put that away. (*As they continue to pick up and put away.*)

GLORIA. You won't tell Sam, will you?

SUSY. Just tell me what's broken. Go on—don't be afraid.

GLORIA. Oh, nothing's broken. I only threw *unbreakables*.

SUSY. Well! That was *crafty* of you. Who taught you that?

GLORIA. Daddy.

SUSY. Oh! Does he throw things sometimes?

GLORIA. (*Cheerfully.*) Boy he sure did the night he left. He went around the whole apartment throwing all the unbreakables on the floor. But Mother finally got wise to this and said "Well—just look at *you!* You can't even *break* anything!" And when we woke up the next morning he'd gone . . . (*Susy is about to pick up a small sharp knife from the table.*) *Look out!* . . . Oh—*I'm sorry, Susy.*

SUSY. That's okay—what is it?

GLORIA. It's just a small kitchen knife—looks sharp. (*Susy feels around carefully and picks it up.*)

SUSY. It is! Thanks . . . (*Front doorbell rings.*) Who is it? (*Doorbell rings again.*) Come in! The door's open.

GLORIA. I'll go to the A & P.

SUSY. Thanks, honey. No rush. (*Gloria picks up list and money and runs up stairs. Doorbell rings again.*) *Come in!*

GLORIA. I'll get it. (*About to open door.*) You can call me Four-Eyes one day if you like . . . but not just yet, if you don't mind. (*Gloria opens door, revealing a man of about seventy standing outside. We may not immediately recognize him as "Roat," who is now disguised as "Harry Roat, Sr." He is eccentric in appearance and manner, even a little crazy. He wears a hat over white, tousled hair. His voice is old and husky.*)

ROAT. I would like to speak to Mr. Sam Hunt.

SUSY. I beg your pardon . . . ? Who are you, please . . . ?

ROAT. Where is she? . . . Where is Mrs. Roat? (*Roat comes inside the door and Gloria stands outside watching him.*)

SUSY. I think you must have the wrong house . . . I'm Mrs. Hendrix . . . who are you please? . . . You see I'm . . .

ROAT. May I have a glass of water? I—I'm not feeling too well.

SUSY. (*Hesitates.*) Okay. Just a minute. (*Susy goes to the sink to find a glass while Roat closes the door. He then starts down the stairs.*) If you'll just wait there, I'll bring it. (*Roat runs into the bedroom and we hear him open several drawers in the dresser.*) What—what are you doing in there? (*After a few moments Roat bursts out of the bedroom. He is brandishing what looks like a thin leather volume [i.e., closed leather framed wedding photograph]. He crosses to Susy like a maniac and as though he does not realize she is blind.*)

ROAT. And you can tell *Sam Hunt*—if he doesn't leave her alone —I'll kill him! (*He starts crossing to door, Mike enters without knocking, and comes down the stairs.*)

MIKE. (*Cheerfully.*) Hello . . . It's Mike Talman again. Sorry— but I think I must have left a package . . . oh yes, there it is—

SUSY. Mike—stop him . . . I don't know who he is . . . (*Roat starts up stairs.*)

MIKE. You just hold it! Who are you? (*Mike pretends to be pushed over so that he falls down the stairs.*)

ROAT. Don't touch me! Don't you dare touch me! I've found it! I've found it in the House of Sin! (*Roat exits, running. Mike gets up from floor.*)

MIKE. Now wait a minute! Come back here! (*Offstage we hear Roat shouting, L.*)

ROAT. Taxi! . . . Taxi!

SUSY. Mike?

MIKE. What happened?

SUSY. (*Scared to death.*) I don't know . . . he just barged in and went into the bedroom. I heard a lot of noise and then . . .

MIKE. And then he emptied your dresser all over the floor . . . I'll call the police.

SUSY. (*Thinking hard.*) The number is . . . 440-1234. . . . Mike, what will I do if he comes back? (*He crosses to the phone, takes out his little notebook and is referring to the telephone number of the phone booth outside.*)

MIKE. 440-1234. (*As he dials the number from his notebook.*) Don't worry, Susy. I'll take a later flight to Phoenix. I'll stay here 'til Sam gets back. Okay?

SUSY. (*With great relief as she sinks onto settee.*) Oh, yes! Thank you.

CURTAIN

END OF ACT I—SCENE 2

ACT I

SCENE 3

TIME: *Twenty minutes later.*

ALTERATIONS TO SET: *Hall door is closed. Venetian blinds are nearly closed downward slant.*

ON RISE: *Carlino enters from bedroom, notebook in hand. He is now dressed as a city police detective and wears raincoat (his hat is on the safe). He is followed by Susy and Mike. Mike is acting as though he is already irritated by Carlino and there is friction between them throughout this scene.*

(Author's Note: During this scene Mike and Carlino occasionally throw each other a glance, but they do not need to overdo this. They have played this con-game together many times with women who are not blind and they tend to behave as though Susy can see. The only exception to this is that Carlino does wipe off a few finger-prints from last night and, being clumsy by nature, he makes more noise than is necessary and Susy notices this once or twice and looks a little puzzled. Carlino has a leather glove on his left hand [which he wears during rest of play] and a handkerchief in his right hand.)

MIKE. *(Annoyed, entering from bedroom.)* But I've got to fly to Phoenix tonight.

CARLINO. Well, maybe that little girl will be able to identify him. Just write your address down here, will you? *(Mike takes Carlino's notebook and writes.)* How many apartments are there in this house—Mrs. Hendrix?

SUSY. Only two, this one and the one upstairs.

CARLINO. *(To Mike, as he wipes off some fingerprints.)* You say he was waving something in his hand, Mr. Talman?

MIKE. *(Still writing in notebook.)* Yes, it looked like a thin leather book . . . here's my address. *(Mike gives notebook back to Carlino. In doing this he points to both sides of the page and Carlino nods. Carlino goes to window and signals with the Venetian blinds, saying to Susy:)*

CARLINO. Excuse me, Mrs. Hendrix, it's a little dark in here . . . this your permanent address, Mr. Talman?

MIKE. Yes it is. *(Susy goes to light switch by bedroom and feels the top switch, finding it is in the "on" position she looks puzzled.)*

CARLINO. *(Picks up hat and goes upstairs.)* Well I won't bother you any more . . . and don't worry, Mrs. Hendrix—if your husband does find anything missing he'll let me know, I'm sure.

SUSY. Yes, he will. And thank you for coming so quickly.

CARLINO. You're entirely welcome. *(The phone rings. Mike*

waves to Carlino to go and he exits, closing door. Susy is near to the phone and picks it up.)

SUSY. Hello . . . yes . . . just a moment please. *(Calling.)* Sergeant Carlino!

MIKE. I'll get him. *(Calling.)* Sergeant! You're wanted on the phone. *(Carlino enters, runs down the stairs and takes phone from Susy.)*

CARLINO. Sorry, Mrs. Hendrix. This is going to be one of those days. *(Into phone.)* Carlino . . . yes, Lieutenant. *(Surprised.)* You mean he just walked in? *(A pause.)* A *doll?* *(A long pause. Susy, who has reacted on the word "doll," is listening hard. Mike and Carlino notice this and glance at each other.)* . . . Have you told him yet? . . . Give me a few minutes. *(A pause.)* Sure, I understand. *(Carlino hangs up. A pause.)*

SUSY. Did they find that old man?

CARLINO. Mrs. Hendrix, maybe I should mention one thing while I'm here. I didn't want to alarm you but a woman was found just outside here this morning . . .

SUSY. Yes, I know.

CARLINO. *(Surprised.)* You say—you *knew* her?

SUSY. Oh no. I just heard about it on the radio.

CARLINO. Oh, I see . . . your *husband* didn't know her by any chance?

SUSY. *(Surprised.)* No.

MIKE. *(Annoyed.)* Of course he didn't.

CARLINO. I'm sorry, Mr. Talman, but we've been told to make inquiries . . . did you hear anything peculiar last night? . . . Mrs. Hendrix?

SUSY. *(Turning.)* No we didn't . . . but we were out most of the evening.

CARLINO. Oh I see—and you and Mr. Hendrix were *together* all evening—I suppose?

SUSY. No. I went to a movie for about an hour while he was working at his studio.

CARLINO. Was anyone else with him?

MIKE. Hey? What is this?

SUSY. No . . . he was supposed to have photographed someone but she never . . .

MIKE. *(To Carlino, angrily.)* Are you questioning Mrs. Hendrix for any particular reason?

34

CARLINO. I'm not questioning her, Mr. Talman.

MIKE. Then why are you taking notes?

SUSY. Mike! . . .

CARLINO. I am *not* taking notes . . . I was only checking to see . . .

MIKE. What?

CARLINO. If there was anything else I *did* want to ask . . .

MIKE. Well if there is I suggest you wait till Mr. Hendrix returns home.

CARLINO. Now look—I am allowed to talk, aren't I?

MIKE. Talk, yes. But Mrs. Hendrix doesn't have to answer any questions if she doesn't want to and if they didn't teach you that at police school read the Constitution.

CARLINO. Okay, then—no more questions. (*Carlino goes upstairs. He turns at door—determined to have a last dig at Mike.*)

MIKE. Have they found that old man yet?

CARLINO. (*With mock respect.*) Mr. Talman, you're not a lawyer by any chance?

MIKE. No—I'm not but . . .

CARLINO. (*With a mocking laugh.*) No—I didn't think you were! (*He exits quickly and closes door. We hear him go down hall and street door slam.*)

MIKE. Well a fat lot of help he was! . . . That old man could be in New Jersey by now . . .

SUSY. (*Interrupting.*) Mike—is this room very dirty?

MIKE. No . . . why?

SUSY. That Sergeant kept dusting everything . . . didn't you notice?

MIKE. No—did he?

SUSY. All around the refrigerator—and in that corner . . . (*Points to safe. The doorbell rings. Susy starts towards it.*)

MIKE. I'll get it. He's probably thought of some more silly questions. (*Mike goes upstairs and opens door. Roat is standing outside. He is now playing the part of Harry Roat Junior, a henpecked square of about forty and quite humorless. He wears a well-cut business suit and eyeglasses [rimless]. Seeing Susy he removes his hat, revealing a middle-aged haircut [or is it a wig?]. He appears out of breath and in a hurry.*)

ROAT. Good afternoon, Mr. . . . Hunt?

MIKE. No . . . Mr. and Mrs. Hendrix live here.

ROAT. *Hendrix?* I beg your pardon. (*Refers to slip of paper in his hand.*) But this *is* 27B Grogan Street?

MIKE. Yes, but . . .

ROAT. My name is Roat. Harry Roat, Junior. May I ask if an elderly gentleman dropped by today?

MIKE. Well! I don't know if he "dropped by" exactly, he . . .

ROAT. Mr. Hendrix—if I may come in for a moment . . . you see, that was my *father*.

SUSY. Yes—come in please.

ROAT. Thank you. (*Roat enters but remains at top of stairs. On his way down, Mike turns to Roat.*)

MIKE. (*Quietly.*) Mr. Roat . . . Mrs. Hendrix is blind.

ROAT. Oh . . . I understand, thank you. (*Roat comes down the stairs. Then, as he approaches Susy she suddenly recoils. This is an instinctive movement of fear and both men notice it and glance at each other.*)

SUSY. Mike!

MIKE. (*Going to her.*) Yes? . . . You all right?

SUSY. Yes, I'm sorry . . . (*Still apprehensive.*) Mr. Roat?

ROAT. I'm so very sorry this happened, Mrs. Hendrix. I do hope my father wasn't *rude* in any way?

MIKE. Well, now—he opened all the drawers in the bedroom. Was that rude, do you think? (*Roat seems to treat this rather lightly.*)

ROAT. Oh my goodness! But let me reassure you—this is not as serious a matter as you may think, Mr. Hendrix.

MIKE. My name is *Talman*—I'm a friend of Mr. Hendrix.

ROAT. Mr. Talman—my father may appear a little—erratic at times but I assure you he would never . . .

MIKE. (*Overlapping.*) Harm anyone?

ROAT. Certainly not.

MIKE. But he just told Mrs. Hendrix that if . . . (*Mike breaks off as Gloria suddenly enters at hall door, without knocking. She is carrying a large grocery bag.*)

SUSY. Gloria!

GLORIA. It's only your groceries. I'll come back later.

SUSY. Leave them *now* if you like. (*Susy moves towards the stairs, bumping into Roat. Gloria doesn't answer but looks from one man to the other with considerable interest. Mike turns his back to her so that she can't see his face. Roat however turns around and looks straight at her deliberately. She then exits.*)

36

ROAT. (*To Mike.*) What did my father say?

MIKE. That if *somebody* didn't leave some woman alone—he would *kill* him!

ROAT. (*More interested than shocked.*) Did he mention the name *Sam Hunt*?

SUSY. Yes! I think that's what he said . . .

ROAT. Ah! Then I can explain all this quite easily. You see my father came here because he thinks your husband is a photographer named *Sam Hunt*.

SUSY. Well—as you see—my husband *is* a photographer but we can clear all this up right away. Mike—there's a picture of Sam and me on the dresser—a *wedding* photograph. (*As Mike reaches bedroom door.*)

ROAT. I'm afraid that won't help *me* very much . . . (*Mike turns in doorway.*) You see *I* have never seen this man.

MIKE. Well just who *is* he, anyway?

ROAT. About three years ago my wife was on vacation in Montreal and while she was there—*my father tells me*—she and this man became . . . acquainted.

MIKE. So your wife meets some guy three years ago—and now your father threatens to *kill* him! For what?

ROAT. My father alleges that they have been seeing each other— from time to time—ever since. (*A pause.*) And now if you'll excuse me, Mrs. Hendrix—I must find my father. (*He moves to stairs.*)

MIKE. (*Puzzled.*) Mr. Roat, before you go—there's one thing I don't quite understand . . . how did *you* get here? (*A pause.*) Did you follow your father here *today*?

ROAT. Er—in a way—yes I did. (*Impatient to leave he opens hall door.*)

MIKE. But . . .

SUSY. Then! . . . (*Puzzled.*) Then you were waiting outside? All the time he was in here? (*No reply.*) Why didn't you stop him?

ROAT. I er—I didn't follow him here *exactly* . . .

MIKE. Then how *exactly* did *you* know this address? (*A long pause.*)

ROAT. I was hoping not to have to tell you this . . .

SUSY. (*Quickly.*) *Please* tell us!

ROAT. (*Slowly.*) I believe my father followed my *wife* to this apartment. (*A pause. Susy does not believe—more angry than hurt.*)

SUSY. When? (*As he talks he comes down the stairs and, step by step, nearer and nearer to Susy.*)

ROAT. Last Sunday my father had invited us to dinner at his club. My wife arrived late and said she couldn't stay because she had to call on a *friend* who was flying to Montreal the next day and she had to give him something. Then my father became very testy and wanted to know his *name* and what it *was* she had to give him and she finally became annoyed and said "Well, if you *must* know —it's that *doll* of mine—that *you* broke!" (*Slight pause.*) Then she got up and walked out . . .

SUSY. A doll—did you say? (*Roat catches Mike's eye but speaks on as if it was of no importance.*)

ROAT. Yes, it was a musical doll. (*A pause. Susy just can't believe it yet, i.e. more curious than hurt.*)

SUSY. Was it . . . ?

ROAT. Yes?

SUSY. You say Mrs. Roat was going to give a doll to—a *friend* —who was going to Canada?

ROAT. Yes.

SUSY. Last . . . Monday?

ROAT. (*Quietly, he is now close to Susy.*) That's right.

SUSY. *Why* did she have to do that?

ROAT. Because this doll wasn't just a toy. It had been specially made for her in Montreal. It played a little tune that was a favorite of hers. (*Whistles tune.*) So her friend said he would take it back to the makers and have it fixed. And then bring it back to her. . . . The moment my wife walked out on us that night my father said to me "It's that doll Sam *Hunt* gave her." Then he followed her. The next morning I found this note under my door— (*He makes a signal with the Venetian blind. Susy reacts to this slightly. Then, while pretending to read from a slip of paper he rustles it so she can hear.*) It just says— (*Reading.*) "Dear Harry—Sam Hunt lives at 27B Grogan Street in Greenwich Village—Dad." (*A pause. Susy now believes and looks as though she has been hit in the stomach. As she moves back her chair her hand nearly knocks over the flower vase [or whatever]. The two men keep glancing from window to the phone as if they expect it to ring any moment.*)

Then, this morning, when I told him that Liciana hadn't come home last night—

SUSY. Who? . . . *Who*—who didn't come home last night?

ROAT. Liciana—my *wife*. But she frequently comes to Manhattan and then decides to stay with friends. She usually phones to say where she is but so far we haven't . . . heard anything. (*The phone rings. Mike starts towards it but Roat holds up his hand and then points to Susy [i.e. "let her take it"]. But Susy is in a daze and doesn't seem to hear the phone. Mike looks back at Roat and shrugs. Roat nods.*)

MIKE. Shall I get it, Susy? (*She does not reply so he picks it up. Mike, into phone:*) Hello . . . one moment. Susy—it's Sergeant Carlino—he wants to speak to you . . . Susy?

SUSY. (*Still dazed.*) Hmmm? . . . What does he want?

ROAT. I must go now, Mrs. Hendrix. (*He starts up the stairs.*)

MIKE. (*Into phone.*) Hello . . . can I take a message? . . . No, I'll take it. Hang on a moment—his *son* is here now . . . Mr. Roat! Don't go—he wants to speak to you.

ROAT. Who?

MIKE. The police . . .

ROAT. (*Alarmed.*) No! . . . (*In a whisper.*) Say I've gone. (*Goes to door.*)

MIKE. But it's about your *wife* . . . (*Susy reacts.*)

ROAT. What? (*He closes door and starts down the stair.*)

MIKE. And your father is at the police station. (*Roat takes phone from Mike.*)

ROAT. Hello . . . speaking . . . that's right . . . no, she didn't but . . . (*A long pause.*) is she hurt? . . . (*Angrily.*) No, tell me *now!* (*Roat listens for several seconds. Then he seems to go into a kind of trance. Susy senses that something is wrong and stands still trying to listen to other end of phone. Finally Roat drops the phone on the table [without hanging up] and runs out of the apartment.*)

MIKE. (*Shouting after him.*) Mr. Roat . . . Mr. Roat! (*Roat exits, leaving hall door open and runs out by the street door. We see him run past the window. Meanwhile Mike hangs up the phone and goes upstairs to close the hall door.*)

SUSY. Mike! Don't go!

MIKE. Of course not. He left the door open. (*As he closes door and comes downstairs he says lightly:*) Well—that's some family, the Roats! The old man just walked into Carlino's office . . . and it seems that *Mrs*. Roat has been in some kind of accident . . .

SUSY. (*Quietly.*) She's dead.

MIKE. What?

SUSY. (*Slowly.*) She was murdered just outside here last night.

MIKE. (*Amazed.*) You *knew* that? . . . All the time he was here?

SUSY. I only realized when he spoke on the phone just now. The Sergeant must have told him. It was on the radio. I think they even mentioned her name only I wasn't listening properly. Mike— could you phone the bus station at Asbury Park . . . and ask them to get Sam to phone me immediately.

MIKE. Sure I will . . . but look—you're not worrying about anything that old man is going to say? He's obviously nuts!

SUSY. But there's something you don't know, Mike . . . Sam *did* bring a child's doll back from Canada . . . (*A pause. She is trying to remember. Mike waits for her to continue.*)

MIKE. But it *can't* be the same one.

SUSY. *Exactly* like the one he described just now. I was trying to help him unpack and I must have knocked it off the bed because it played a few notes. So I picked it up and said, "Ah, surprise!" or something like that. I thought it was a present for me. But Sam said— (*Trying to remember.*) he said—no, it was for a little girl who was in a hospital . . . some *woman* he'd met at the airport in Montreal had asked him to bring it here for her . . . *someone* . . . someone he said he'd never met before . . . (*Her voice trails away as she realizes that Sam must have been lying.*)

MIKE. (*Coaxing her gently.*) And so—Sam took it to the hospital . . . ?

SUSY. No—this woman . . . *it must have been Mrs. Roat!* She came here late that night to pick it up but—but Sam couldn't find it . . . *it must still be here somewhere.* (*Becoming hysterical.*) And that Italian woman who didn't turn up last night . . . Liciana. That was Mrs. Roat too! (*Susy rushes into bedroom, feels on dresser, knocking over some bottles.*)

MIKE. Now just take it easy, Susy. Suppose Sam *did* know her, that's not so serious . . .

SUSY. (*Comes out of bedroom.*) Mike—can you see a photograph of Sam and me—it should be on the dresser? It's a wedding photograph in a leather frame— (*Mike peers through doorway.*)

MIKE. Not on the dresser . . . (*Suddenly.*) Oh, that's what the old man was carrying when he left the house . . .

SUSY. (*Slowly, overlapping.*) He's taken a photograph of *Sam* to the police . . .

MIKE. (*Going to phone.*) Then let's phone Carlino and tell him.

SUSY. *No!* We mustn't say *anything* to the police. The Sergeant mentioned a doll when he was on the phone, don't you remember? And all those questions about where Sam was last night—and about the murdered woman—the police must think he . . . they must think he killed her! (*Mike is already standing on stool—he flicks the blinds loudly as though looking out of window.*)

MIKE. Susy!

SUSY. What is it?

MIKE. (*Quietly.*) There's a police car just down the street . . . (*A long pause—he turns and watches her.*) They're watching this house.

CURTAIN

END ACT I—SCENE 3

ACT II

SCENE 1

TIME: *About an hour later.*

ALTERATIONS TO SET: *The clock shows . . . The Venetian blinds are both closed. There is visual evidence that Susy and Mike have made a thorough search of the apartment during the last hour. A vacuum cleaner, broom, etc. lie outside the closet under the stairs and the closets under the sink, etc., have been emptied out into the room. (But the facade is still hiding the safe and Sam's steel file is still locked.)*

ON RISE: *Mike is alone on stage. His jacket is off, etc., and he appears tired and frustrated. He looks at his watch and then, with a glance at the bedroom, he goes to window and makes a signal with one of the blinds—leaving it closed. Then he goes straight to the telephone and waits. There is the noise of a table lamp falling over in the bedroom and an angry cry, off, from Susy. Mike looks at phone and then gestures impatiently towards Venetian blinds.*

MIKE. Come on! (*The phone rings. Mike grabs it. Into phone:*) Hello . . . yes . . . yes it is . . . (*Calling to Susy in bedroom.*) Asbury Park—bus station.

SUSY. (*Calling, off.*) Let me speak to him.

MIKE. (*Into phone.*) He caught the five o'clock bus from Manhattan . . . are you *sure?* . . . (*To Susy.*) He wasn't on it . . .

SUSY. (*Hurrying out of bedroom.*) But he *must* have been . . .

MIKE. Maybe he missed it.

SUSY. If he had he'd have phoned. Let me speak to them! (*She runs forward violently towards the phone and runs straight into a small table knocking it over and falling hard onto the floor.*)

MIKE. (*He bangs up phone and goes to Susy.*) You okay, Susy? (*He tries to help her up.*)

SUSY. (*In complete despair.*) No! (*He leaves her alone.*) That does it! . . . That's the third time in half an hour and I just broke a lamp in the bedroom. (*Mike tries again to help her up.*)

MIKE. Let me help you up then . . .

SUSY. No, leave me alone! It's no good, Mike. I can't.

MIKE. If you could at least remember where Sam keeps the key of that filing cabinet.

SUSY. We'll just have to wait for Sam to get back—I just can't understand why he hasn't phoned by now.

MIKE. We can't wait for Sam. We've got to find that doll and destroy it and anything else that might connect Sam and Mrs. Roat. And *before* that Sergeant comes back. If we don't . . .

SUSY. (*Suddenly.*) Back of the freezer!

MIKE. What do you mean—back of the freezer?

SUSY. (*Getting up from floor.*) The key of the filing cabinet! I knew it was a funny place. (*Mike rushes to refrigerator and finds the small key frozen to the back of the freezer.*) Is it there?

MIKE. Yes—it's frozen in. (*He hacks at it with his razor blade.*)

SUSY. There should be a twenty-dollar bill there too . . . do you see it?

MIKE. (*With a glance round at her.*) Yes—I see it. (*A lie.*)

SUSY. We put that there when we moved in here . . . in case we ever starved to death. (*Mike goes to filing cabinet and unlocks it and rapidly searches first two drawers.*) Is the doll there?

MIKE. No—but this is. (*Mike takes out a cardboard box [of keys] from bottom drawer, opens it and hands it to Susy.*)

SUSY. (*Quickly.*) Now we're off! These are all the keys we have. There's one for everything that's locked. There should be a small key on a large paper clip—with a tag. (*Mike finds it.*)

MIKE. "Small suitcase"?

SUSY. That's it. That's where Sam keeps important papers and stuff. (*She takes it and feels her way into the bedroom, as she exits:*) Thanks, Mike—I'm feeling better now. (*As soon as she has gone Mike picks out two or three of the larger keys, throwing glances at the safe. Then he goes to safe and, quietly opening the facade, tries each of the keys in its lock. He freezes still as Susy enters from bedroom. She is carrying the suitcase and the key.*) Mike?

MIKE. (*Moving away from safe.*) Here, Susy.

SUSY. (*Giving him key and suitcase.*) Would you open this? (*Mike unlocks and opens case and pretends to search.*) Well—is

43

the doll in there? (*No reply. Susy then feels around in case and finds a bundle of letters with a rubber band around them.*)

MIKE. No doll. (*Susy hands him the letters.*)

SUSY. Here, maybe you'd better look these over, just in case. (*Mike glances at the back of each envelope, checking the return address. Susy waits anxiously.*) Can you see all right? (*Her hand feels the light switch by bedroom door.*)

MIKE. (*Puzzled.*) See what?

SUSY. To read the letters.

MIKE. Oh, sure. The light is on. (*He resumes checking letters.*)

SUSY. If any of them are from her—don't read them to me just— just burn them in the sink. (*He looks round at the sink and then at Susy as she waits. [He is tempted—this would really clinch it.] He takes a step towards the sink. Susy, trying not to appear frightened:*) Well? (*Mike turns from sink and puts letters in her hand.*)

MIKE. They're all from you, Susy . . . you type pretty well. (*Note: This is Susy's real turning point—from here on she picks up.*)

SUSY. Oh! Well that's a relief! I didn't know Sam was a hoarder! I nearly didn't show them to you. (*Pause.*) And you haven't found anything yet? . . . Of hers? (*As Mike talks he crosses to the safe.*)

MIKE. Not yet. And we've looked in just about every place it could be . . . everywhere except this safe . . . I only just noticed it was here. (*But Susy has her attention elsewhere and has moved back to the light switch.*)

SUSY. This is the light that hangs down from the ceiling? (*She switches it off and then on, from door.*)

MIKE. Yes, it is.

SUSY. On now?

MIKE. On . . . why?

SUSY. It's nothing . . . only I noticed that Carlino had to open the blinds to read something. And yet this switch was on. I felt it.

MIKE. Well, they're on now anyway. Do you think Sam could have put that doll in this safe? . . . (*A pause. He is watching her carefully. but she hardly seems to be listening.*) Susy?

SUSY. Hmmm? In the safe? (*Casually.*) No, it couldn't be in there. (*Slowly.*) . . . And Mr. Roat did the same thing.

MIKE. (*Impatiently.*) Did *what?*

44

SUSY. He opened the blinds too—didn't he?

MIKE. Did he?

SUSY. Well, I presume he didn't *close* them! . . . Mike, did you notice how I kind of *jumped* when Roat Junior came down the stairs?

MIKE. Yes—why?

SUSY. For a moment I thought it was the old man. (*A long pause.*)

MIKE. You mean—that they were *together*?

SUSY. Yes. Of course I realized right away I was wrong but he had exactly the same walk as his father . . . (*Quietly.*) and the same shoes. (*Pause.*)

MIKE. (*With a laugh.*) You mean they *sounded* the same . . .

SUSY. But *exactly* the same. New shoes and one of them squeaked a bit. *You* probably didn't notice . . .

MIKE. No I didn't.

SUSY. You're wearing old loafers . . . (*Mike looks down at his shoes.*) Sam wears them most of the time. . . . Is that police car still outside? (*Mike hesitates, then goes to window, climbs on stool and pretends to look through blinds.*)

MIKE. (*Looking at Susy.*) Yes it is . . . and they're looking this way.

SUSY. Can you see their faces?

MIKE. (*Still looking at Susy.*) Not too well.

SUSY. Try! . . . This is *very* important!

MIKE. Why?

SUSY. This may surprise you, Mike. (*Slowly.*) But is one of those men—*Mr. Roat*? (*He stares at her a long time.*)

MIKE. Mr. *Roat*?!

SUSY. Well? Is it? (*A pause.*)

MIKE. The old man—or the son?

SUSY. (*After a pause.*) Roat Junior. (*A pause.*)

MIKE. No . . . now *what* would he be doing in a police car?

SUSY. (*Still excited.*) There's a radio in that car, isn't there?

MIKE. I don't know. Suppose there is? (*As Susy quickly fires her questions, Mike is looking at her curiously and becomes increasingly cautious as he wonders how near to the truth she is guessing.*)

SUSY. (*Slowly.*) I'm just wondering if . . . do you think *Mr. Roat* could possibly be a policeman too? (*A pause. Mike breathes more freely, delighted that she is so wide of the mark.*)

MIKE. (*Almost amused.*) What—*what* makes you think *that*?

SUSY. (*Faster.*) First of all Carlino fiddles with those blinds and almost immediately the police phone and ask to speak to him . . . then Roat fiddles with them . . . and then Carlino phones *him* . . .

MIKE. He didn't. He phoned *you*.

SUSY. (*Wondering to herself.*) Or did he?

MIKE. (*As though he thinks her idea ridiculous.*) Oh, I see. You mean sending each other messages—via these blinds? And the police radio?

SUSY. (*Hoping to convince him.*) *Something* like that. You must admit—if they did suspect Sam—it would be a pretty neat trick . . . when Roat first mentioned that doll—I nearly told him all about it. (*Mike gets off stool and crosses to settee.*)

MIKE. I doubt if the police work like *that*.

SUSY. You see, I *know* Mr. Roat's story and Sam's just don't match . . . but I'd forgotten something. (*A pause.*)

MIKE. What?

SUSY. That I *know* Sam. And I don't know Mr. Roat at all! Do I?

MIKE. (*Strongly.*) Look, Susy, if Sam can explain all this—fine. Then there's nothing to worry about. But if he *can't*—*I* want to help him . . . Susy—why don't you want to tell me about *this safe*? (*As she talks, she returns letters to suitcase, closes it and puts it on floor in front of settee.*)

SUSY. (*Lightly.*) Oh it can't be in there because . . . well—it just isn't *ours*. You see the woman who had this apartment before us . . . she tried to sell it to us for two hundred dollars. Then one hundred—then fifty . . . and when we finally made it clear that we just didn't want it—she *locked* it . . . and then she walked out and Sam saw her deliberately drop the key down the drain outside. (*A pause. Mike watches her very suspiciously.*)

MIKE. Susy, are you making this up?

SUSY. Of course not! . . . Why should I?

MIKE. (*With a laugh.*) Not that I blame you. I don't think I would open up my safe in front of a complete stranger—even if I could watch him. (*He picks up his jacket from back of chair and puts it on.*)

SUSY. Now have I been treating you like a complete stranger?

MIKE. No but . . .

SUSY. I just wish that doll *was* in the safe! Then *nobody* could find it—could they?

MIKE. (*After a pause.*) I wouldn't count on that. If the police get a warrant to search this place, and they may, they could have it opened up . . . have you thought of that?

SUSY. Open this safe? Without a key?

MIKE. They could drill it open.

SUSY. (*Delighted.*) Well—let's hope they try! That would take *hours*, wouldn't it? *And by that time Sam will be home!* (*A long pause. Mike realizes he is getting nowhere and decides to try something else.*)

MIKE. I guess you're right . . . but you'd better make *sure* if it's in there.

SUSY. You really believe . . . !

MIKE. Not now—but when I've gone. (*He picks up raincoat and goes upstairs.*)

SUSY. (*Alarmed.*) You're going? . . . Where?

MIKE. To the apartment—where I've been staying.

SUSY. Why?

MIKE. Just to pick up my things. I'll bring them over here.

SUSY. But do you have to go *now*?

MIKE. (*Smoothly.*) Someone else is moving in there tonight and I have to return the key. I won't be long. (*He moves to exit. Susy is discouraged and on the downs again. As he reaches the door she says:*)

SUSY. Then you better give me your phone number.

MIKE. (*Turning.*) *What* phone number?

SUSY. Where you're going now. (*A pause.*)

MIKE. But it's just round the corner . . . (*Susy starts to find jar of sugar lumps.*)

SUSY. But if you're delayed . . . and in case I *do* find the doll.

MIKE. I—I'll phone you when I get there. (*He turns to go.*)

SUSY. (*Impatiently.*) Then, just give me the *name* of your friends —or the *address* . . . so I can call Information. (*A pause. Mike is now in a corner. Then he takes out his notebook.*)

MIKE. I—er—I just *may* have it written down *somewhere* . . . (*Checking number from his notebook.*) Yes, here it is . . . but can you *remember* it?

SUSY. Sure I can—just a second. (*She goes to phone and takes out handful of sugar lumps.*) . . . Ready.

MIKE. (*Slowly.*) W—A—4 . . .

SUSY. (*Quickly.*) That's 924—same as this one. Go on.

MIKE. 5 . . . 3 . . . 0 . . . 9. (*With great concentration, she goes into her muttering routine as though chanting a prayer to the god of numbers.)*

SUSY. 5309 . . . oh, that's a stinker! . . . Five-thirty-nine . . . *(Then very rapidly.)* . . . there's always one magic number . . . I'll be thirty in two years—that's *almost* three, isn't it? Three threes are nine. And twice three is six except it's *five* and not six. So it's THREE. *(She places three sugar lumps by phone.)* O.K.— 924—*FIVE*—thirty, I mean three zero . . . nine . . . 5309?

MIKE. *(Amazed.)* That's right! How long can you remember that?

SUSY. About two and a half minutes. *So hurry! (Mike opens hall door.)* Oh!—And lock the street door in case Carlino comes back and this one too—I'll let you in. *(Mike slips catch on the door to lock it.)*

MIKE. O.K.—locked. *(Starts to exit.)*

SUSY. And Mike . . .

MIKE. *(Turns back.)* Yes?

SUSY. I just don't know *what* I'd have done if you hadn't come by today. *(Mike looks down at Susy a moment. He has never felt such a heel in his life. He tries to say something, then gives up and exits, closing door. We hear him walk to street door and lock it and then walk to the back door and slam it shut as he leaves house. Susy finds suitcase and takes it into bedroom. The stage is empty for several seconds, then we hear someone try the handle of hall door. Long pause. Then a key is fitted into the lock and Gloria creeps in. She is carrying the same large grocery bag that she had before. Seeing no one in the room she tiptoes down the stairs. She glances through open bedroom door then opens the grocery bag and takes out the doll. As though she has already thought this out, she puts the doll carefully on the floor under the side table by settee [i.e. as though it had fallen there by accident]. Then she creeps back up the stairs. When halfway up Susy enters from bedroom. Gloria freezes still but she is too late and Susy hears her.)* Who is that . . . Mike?

GLORIA. *(Turning on stairs.)* Oh, hello, Susy!

SUSY. *(Startled.)* Oh! Don't *do* that to me! How did you get in here?

GLORIA. I borrowed the key you lent Mother. Because when I got upstairs I found I'd left a stick of butter in the bottom of the bag . . . *(Susy puts out her hand.)*

48

SUSY. Thank you, honey.

GLORIA. It's already in the icebox. I closed the door. You can pay me tomorrow, if you like. It came to four seventy-two, but you owe me thirty-five cents from last time so if I give you thirteen . . . (*Susy puts her hands up to her ears.*)

SUSY. Don't! No more numbers, please, I'm not a computer. Just call it quits—O.K.?

GLORIA. O.K.—Thanks. Bye-bye, then. (*Gloria pauses above settee on way to stairs.*) It's none of my business but that man who was in here with Sam's friend . . .

SUSY. That was a Mr. Roat . . . yes? . . . What about him?

GLORIA. Is he a detective?

SUSY. (*Very interested.*) Why? . . . What makes you *think* he is?

GLORIA. Because of the lady who was murdered last night—that's all. (*A pause. Susy goes to kitchen stool.*)

SUSY. Look, honey, if you stand on this . . . can you see through the window? (*Gloria climbs up on stool and as she isn't high enough she stands on top of washer.*)

GLORIA. I think so.

SUSY. There's a police car outside . . . (*No reply.*) You see it?

GLORIA. No.

SUSY. Look carefully—are you sure?

GLORIA. (*Looking through blind of the other window.*) No police car.

SUSY. It must have gone. There was one there a few minutes ago . . . can you see a policeman? . . . *Anywhere?*

GLORIA. No.

SUSY. Or *anyone* who might be watching this house?

GLORIA. Don't think so. Not many people around. It's still raining. (*Pause.*) Can I get down now?

SUSY. Yes, of course . . . (*Gloria starts to climb down.*) Oh, wait a minute. When we first moved in here—Sam used to make his phone calls from a phone booth somewhere out there. I think it was near some traffic lights. Can you see a phone booth from this window? (*Gloria has already climbed up and looks through* D. *window.*)

GLORIA. Yes, there's one by the parking lot at the end of the street.

SUSY. Is there—a car parked anywhere *near* the phone booth?

GLORIA. One of those Volkswagen buses . . . it's right beside it.

SUSY. Anyone in it?

GLORIA. I can't see. It has curtains all around. (*She glances at Susy.*) Is something the matter, Susy? You look awfully worried.

SUSY. It's nothing, honey—I'll be all right when Sam gets home.

GLORIA. Would you like me to stay with you until he . . . (*She is looking through the window again and says casually:*) . . . there's a man getting out now.

SUSY. The Volkswagen?

GLORIA. Yes . . . he's talking to someone inside. I can't *see* who it is . . . now he's coming this way . . .

SUSY. (*Quickly.*) Is it Mr. Roat? . . . That man who you thought was a detective?

GLORIA. No. It isn't. Sam hasn't done anything, has he? (*She jumps off stool. She has left both Venetian blinds open.*)

SUSY. No, of course not . . . Honey, you remember that *doll* your mother asked you about?

GLORIA. What about it? (*As Susy continues talking Carlino appears outside the window and peers in. [The doll is just out of his sight.] But Gloria sees him first and ducks down underneath the settee.*)

SUSY. It belonged to the woman who was killed last night. And if the police found it here they might think that Sam had something to do with it. That's why it's so important . . .

GLORIA. Look out!

SUSY. What is it?

GLORIA. (*In a whisper.*) There's a man looking through the window. (*Susy goes over to sink and pretends to be cleaning up.*)

SUSY. (*Without moving her lips.*) Can he see you?

GLORIA. No . . . but he's still looking . . . it's the man from the Volkswagen. (*Very cautiously Gloria feels for the doll and then drags it carefully behind the settee. As she does this, it plays two or three notes of its tune. Susy hears this and turns sharply. Carlino leaves the window. Gloria peeps cautiously over settee.*)

SUSY. (*Horrified.*) Don't let him see the doll! (*Susy backs to L. wall and closes the blackout across both windows. [See note p. 60.]*)

GLORIA. Now he's gone. (*A pause, then street doorbell rings.*)

SUSY. That's the street door! And it's locked . . . run up and see if you can lock the back door. (*Gloria grabs the doll and runs halfway up the stairs, then halts.*)

50

GLORIA. We can't. I think Daddy took the key with him. (*Street doorbell rings again.*)

SUSY. We've got to hide that doll quickly! *Anywhere!*

GLORIA. (*Running up.*) I'll take it upstairs.

SUSY. No! In here! (*Gloria runs down stairs and stuffs doll back in the grocery bag, twists the top shut and hides it in the garbage pail underneath the other garbage bag.*) Where on earth did you find it?

GLORIA. (*Innocently.*) It was just lying under the table by the settee—I guess it must have fallen off . . .

SUSY. (*Sharply.*) We've been searching this room for over an hour. You've got to tell me.

GLORIA. (*After a pause.*) I took it. (*Street doorbell rings.*)

SUSY. Why?

GLORIA. When I first saw it in here, I thought it was a present for me, but Sam said it was for *another* little girl. So . . . I stole it. It's under the garbage. You can't possibly see it. (*Susy speaks very quickly but with tremendous emphasis.*)

SUSY. How would you like to do something that's difficult—and terribly dangerous?

GLORIA. Yes! . . . *What?*

SUSY. Can you see that phone booth—from *upstairs?*

GLORIA. From Mother's bedroom—I think.

SUSY. (*Pointing to phone.*) Write down our phone number quickly. (*As Gloria goes to phone and copies the number down:*) Now listen very carefully—this is difficult . . . go upstairs and watch that phone booth and don't take your eyes off it. Not for a second. (*Slowly.*) Now if *anyone* from the Volkswagen goes in and makes a phone call—phone me the moment he comes out . . . do you understand?

GLORIA. (*As if it was nothing.*) Sure—I understand.

SUSY. *Only* the Volkswagen people—and *only* after they come *out* of the phone booth.

GLORIA. No problem. (*When Gloria is halfway up the stairs.*)

SUSY. No, wait, I've got a better idea. When you phone me *I won't* answer. Just let it ring *twice*. And then hang up.

GLORIA. (*Coming down to Susy.*) I know. Like a signal. There's a friend of Daddy's who does that. Only *she* does it *seven times.* (*Gloria starts upstairs again, then turns and says in whisper:*)

51

Susy, if you need me for anything just bang on that water pipe. You can hear it all over the house.

SUSY. Where is it?

GLORIA. By the stove. I'll show you. (*She comes down to Susy and starts to lead her to water pipe. During Gloria's last speech we can hear Carlino enter by the back door and then the hall doorbell rings. Susy puts out her hands and holds Gloria by the shoulders to keep her from moving.*)

SUSY. (*Calling.*) Who is it?

CARLINO. (*Off.*) It's Sergeant Carlino.

SUSY. (*Calling.*) Just a second, Sergeant. I'm on the phone. I won't be a moment. (*Gloria pulls Susy's head down, whispers something into her ear. Susy nods and Gloria quietly tiptoes into the closet under the stairs and closes the door. To cover Gloria's movements Susy pretends to be speaking on the phone.*) That's a wonderful idea—and a box of Kleenex and a large bottle of aspirin . . . that's all, honey—I'll have to go now. There's someone at the door . . . bye. (*Susy goes upstairs and opens door. Carlino enters. As she leads him into the bedroom, Susy says:*) I'm sorry I kept you waiting. And I'm so glad you came because some kids were playing out at the back and I think they've broken a window in the bathroom. Would you mind taking a look?

CARLINO. I've got more important things to do, Mrs. Hendrix.

SUSY. It would only take you a moment . . . if you would, please. (*After a very careful glance around the room, Carlino follows Susy into bedroom. Once he is in there Susy backs into the bedroom doorway so that we [and Gloria] can see her.*)

CARLINO. (*Off.*) There's nothing wrong with the bathroom window. (*Gloria peeps out of stair closet, then comes out, closes door and creeps up the stair and exits by hall door. On her way past Susy she pats her on the back. Susy then moves back into bedroom.*)

SUSY. (*Off.*) How about this window then?

CARLINO. (*Off.*) It's okay.

SUSY. (*As she enters.*) Oh—I'm sure I heard some glass breaking somewhere. Well, thanks for looking anyway. Was there something you wanted to ask me?

CARLINO. (*Entering.*) I understand that a Mr. Roat called on you just now.

SUSY. Yes he did.

CARLINO. I thought you should know that the woman who was murdered outside here last night was his wife.

SUSY. Oh.

CARLINO. (*Accusingly.*) You don't seem very surprised to hear that.

SUSY. Well, from the way her husband behaved on the phone I guessed something had happened. (*Carlino moves around the room for several seconds, looking at the open closets, etc.*)

CARLINO. You seem to have been searching for something since I was here last, Mrs. Hendrix.

SUSY. Yes—I was trying to find some bags for the vacuum cleaner.

CARLINO. Oh—some bags for the vacuum cleaner—well, maybe I can find them for you. (*He starts to search in closets, etc.*)

SUSY. No, please don't bother. (*As Carlino talks he searches inside the washing machine, rummaging amongst the clothes and towels.*)

CARLINO. No bother at all . . . you know the other day my wife lost her only can opener . . . and you'll never guess where I found it . . .

SUSY. (*Immediately.*) In the washing machine?

CARLINO. (*Turning, surprised.*) That's right! Just thought you might have done the same thing.

SUSY. Thank you. But I'd rather you didn't look for them now.

CARLINO. Are you sure you weren't looking for something *else*, Mrs. Hendrix? (*No reply.*) Are you sure you weren't looking . . . for a doll?

SUSY. A doll? I don't know what you mean?

CARLINO. A doll that your husband brought back from Canada . . . and which Mrs. Roat came here to collect the other night.

SUSY. My husband never knew Mrs. Roat.

CARLINO. We know he did. Mr. Roat now recognizes your husband from a photograph that his father has.

SUSY. You mean which he *stole* from our bedroom?

CARLINO. And the old man remembers seeing your husband and Mrs. Roat together several times. (*No reply. He crosses slowly to safe, watching Susy closely.*) Now where else might that doll be . . . in this safe perhaps? (*A pause.*)

SUSY. Why would my husband have to put a doll in there?

CARLINO. And if he did *you* couldn't open it anyway, could you?

SUSY. (*After a pause.*) *Yes.* As it so happens, I could.

53

CARLINO. (*Surprised.*) You could?

SUSY. Yes. (*A pause.*)

CARLINO. Then will you open it?

SUSY. For you?

CARLINO. Yes.

SUSY. Now?

CARLINO. Yes.

SUSY. *Certainly not!* You'll need a warrant for that and you know it.

CARLINO. Oh we'll have a warrant in no time.

SUSY. Then you'll have to *blast* it open! You'll get no help from me!

CARLINO. It won't take us twenty minutes to drill that open and *before* your husband gets back. (*He starts to go up the stairs, then turns.*) And in the meantime you are not to leave this house. (*Just as he reaches door.*)

SUSY. Oh, Sergeant—is Mr. Roat still at the Sixth Precinct? (*A pause.*)

CARLINO. (*Surprised.*) He's probably left there by now. Why?

SUSY. I just wanted to tell him something—that is very important . . . could you give me his phone number *please?*

CARLINO. His phone number?

SUSY. Yes. (*A pause.*) Now you're not going to tell me he didn't give it to *you.*

CARLINO. Well of course he did—but I don't have it on me. Maybe you can get it from Information. He lives in Scarsdale.

SUSY. I've already tried and it's not listed. Oh—I know how I can get it. (*She goes to phone and starts to dial.*)

CARLINO. What are you doing?

SUSY. (*As she dials.*) 440-1234. They'll put me through to the Sixth Precinct and *they* can tell me Mr. Roat's phone number. (*As Carlino hurries to phone.*)

CARLINO. Look—that's only for police emergencies—I can dial my office direct. It's just possible he may still be there.

SUSY. Thank you. (*She bangs up. Carlino takes up phone and dials carefully from his notebook.*)

CARLINO. (*Into phone.*) Carlino . . . is Mr. Roat still there? . . . No, the son . . . Mrs. Hendrix wants to speak to him. (*He puts the phone into her hand.*)

SUSY. Thank you. (*Into phone.*) Mr. Roat? . . . My husband's

54

friend, Mr. Talman, has just phoned a lawyer and he has advised us that if your father makes any more accusations against my husband he will take immediate action . . . do you understand what I'm saying? . . . Thank you, Mr. Roat. (*Susy hangs up. Carlino who has been watching her phone with obvious amusement now starts up the stairs.*)

CARLINO. (*As he goes.*) That lawyer friend isn't going to stop me, Mrs. Hendrix. And I'll be right back with . . . (*Just as Carlino reaches the door the phone starts to ring and he turns and starts down the stairs as though expecting that it may be for him. Susy lets it ring exactly twice and then picks it up.*) That might be for me.

SUSY. (*Into phone.*) Hello . . . (*A long pause as she listens. Then, as though puzzled:*) . . . There's no answer . . . they must have hung up. (*She hangs up. Carlino goes again to hall door and opens it.*)

CARLINO. I'll be right back, Mrs. Hendrix—*with a search warrant.*

SUSY. I'll be here. (*Carlino exits, but as he closes the door he slips the catch so that it is not locked. We can hear him walk along the hallway, L., to the street door. We hear it open and slam. Susy immediately goes and feels for the sugar lumps which gave her Mike's phone number. As she dials she mutters rapidly to herself [the same way as she did to Mike].*) Three . . . so it's nine two four . . . not six but five . . . thirty . . . and . . . nine. (*After a pause, into phone.*) Mike? . . . I've got it! . . . The doll! . . . I'll tell you when you get here . . . come right away . . . and Mike . . . I was right about Mr. Roat—he is a detective! He and Carlino have been— (*She breaks off suddenly as she hears the click of the hall door as it opens about six inches. Then she says into phone quietly:*) Hurry! (*She hangs up and calls to the hall door.*) Sergeant Carlino? . . . Did you forget something? (*The door closes quietly. Susy goes quickly upstairs, calling as she goes.*) Sergeant Carlino! (*She opens hall door and taking her blind stick off the railing, goes out into the hallway and waves her stick around [in case he is still there].*) Sergeant Carlino! (*Then she disappears R. [to check the back door] and we hear the street door close . . . [Carlino going out]. While Susy is still off stage, the phone starts to ring again. Susy appears in the doorway at the end of the first ring and comes downstairs quickly to answer it.*)

[*Maybe it's Sam phoning.*] After its second ring, it stops. *Susy's reaction to this is delayed, i.e. she goes on a few paces to the phone and then stops suddenly. She stands there absolutely still for several seconds while the horror of the situation slowly dawns on her:* [*i.e. that Gloria has seen Mike come out of that same phone booth and that he too is working with Carlino and Roat*].) Mike! (*Then in a near panic, she turns and hurries up the stairs and slams the hall door and makes sure it is locked. She tries to hang up her stick but it falls over the railing onto the floor. She runs down the stairs and crosses to the garbage pail and takes out the doll, quickly stuffing the grocery bag and pail back under the sink. Then holding the doll she crosses towards the bedroom but when she is halfway across the room, we hear someone running outside,* R., *and entering the back door and then trying to open the hall door. Then he knocks on door. Susy, calling:*) Who is it?

MIKE. (*Off.*) Mike.

SUSY. (*Calling.*) Just a second, Mike. (*For a moment she doesn't know what to do. Then she takes the doll to the washing machine, opens it and wrapping the doll in a towel, buries it under the washing.*)

MIKE. Susy!

SUSY. I'm coming. (*Then she closes the washer door as quietly as possible and goes up stairs and opens hall door. Mike stands outside. He is out of breath.*) Come in quickly, Mike . . . close the door. (*She turns and goes down the stairs. Mike slams the door, pretending to lock it, but immediately opens it again, very quietly, until it is wide open. He then comes halfway down the stairs and pauses. He is very tense.*)

MIKE. Well? (*Susy turns and faces him but does not reply. A long pause. Then we see Carlino appear silently from* R. *Very quietly he tiptoes into the room and stands motionless on the top stair, staring straight at Susy.*) You've got it? (*A pause.*)

SUSY. (*Quietly.*) Yes. (*A pause. We now see Roat move silently into the doorway, from* R. *He is still dressed as Harry Roat Junior, except that the rimless glasses have been removed and his character seems completely changed and quite sinister. He stares coldly at Susy.*)

MIKE. Well? . . . Where is it? (*During the long pause which follows Susy simply stands there facing the three men as though she*

*just cannot think what to do next. Then, after the long pause, she
calls sharply as though speaking to someone in the hall doorway.)*
SUSY. Gloria?
MIKE. What's the matter?
SUSY. I thought for a moment . . . there was someone else there.
MIKE. *(Very calmly.)* No—it was just the door—didn't quite
close. *(Mike goes up to top of stairs. Roat holds out his hand for
Mike to stop still. Then Roat closes the door himself.)* That's bet-
ter.
SUSY. Is it still raining?
MIKE. Yes . . . *(Impatiently.)* Susy—where is the doll?
SUSY. You'll see—I won't be a second. *(Susy exits into bedroom.
Carlino takes a step down as though to follow her but Mike holds
him back. They all look at each other and decide to wait for her
to return. [Maybe it's in the bedroom!] After several seconds Susy
enters from bedroom wearing a raincoat and carrying a zip purse
slung from one shoulder. She goes straight to the settee and starts
feeling around for something.)*
MIKE. *(Very surprised.)* Where are you going?
SUSY. Where's the box of keys?
MIKE. In front of the settee—is it in the safe? *(Susy finds key
box and holds them out to Mike.)*
SUSY. Can you find three keys on a ring—one large and two
small?
MIKE. Is it . . . in the safe?
SUSY. No . . . but I *did* look there.
MIKE. You did! . . . When?
SUSY. As soon as you had gone.
MIKE. Then all that nonsense about the old woman?
SUSY. Oh—I was just making that up. *(Laughs.)* I thought you
realized. I mean—as you said yourself—I don't know you that
well! You're not hurt, are you?
MIKE. Are those the ones you want? *(He hands Susy three keys
on a ring and she feels them carefully.)*
SUSY. Yes! Good! *(She puts them into her coat pocket and starts
to cross towards sink.)*
MIKE. *(Exasperated.)* Susy! You said you had found the doll!
SUSY. *(Turning.)* I know where it is.
MIKE. Where?

SUSY. It's locked up . . . in Sam's desk. (*Pause. The three men look all around the room and then at each other.*)

MIKE. What desk?

SUSY. In his studio. (*She turns and crosses to kitchen drawer and feels around the draining board for kitchen knife. Mike turns to Roat. Roat's eyes never leave Susy [he believes her—so far]. He makes a hand-winding sign to Mike ["Keep quizzing her"].*)

MIKE. How do you know it's there? (*Susy turns from the sink and faces Mike.*)

SUSY. You remember that little girl who came in when Mr. Roat was here?

MIKE. Yes.

SUSY. She told me. She phoned me from the drug store.

MIKE. (*Bewildered.*) When?

SUSY. Just after you left. She wanted to know if I needed anything and I thought I might as well ask her if *she* had seen the doll anywhere—and by golly she had!

MIKE. When?

SUSY. Yesterday morning. I had sent her to Sam's studio because I needed some money. She often does my shopping for me. And when she walked into his little office at the back—there was the doll on his desk! Of course she thought it was a present for her—just as I had—but Sam said no—it was for *another* little girl. And then he locked it in his desk. (*Mike to Roat—a quick glance.*)

MIKE. (*Suspiciously.*) Strange place to put a doll.

SUSY. (*Without the slightest hesitation.*) That's exactly what she said! "That's a funny place to put a doll! What do you want to lock it up for?"

MIKE. And what did Sam say to that?

SUSY. He said something . . . rather odd!

MIKE. What?

SUSY. He said . . . (*Slowly.*) "Ah! but this is a doll that even grownups would like to have."

MIKE. (*After a pause and another glance at Roat.*) Susy, are you making this up?

SUSY. Go and ask her if you like. She's probably still there. It's the drug store at the corner of Sixth Avenue and Fourth Street. (*Carlino makes a move as though to leave but Roat puts out his hand and stops him. Susy has found kitchen knife. As she crosses to stairs she puts knife in her purse.*)

MIKE. Where are you going with that knife?

SUSY. There's a john at the back of Sam's studio. I'm going to slice that doll up into tiny pieces and flush it away! (*Mike turns to Roat in horror and Carlino looks as though he is about to throw up. Roat, still as cool as steel, prods his finger at Mike ["You go!"]. Mike stops Susy gently from going up the stairs.*)

MIKE. (*Quietly.*) Now just hold it, Susy . . . you can't go!

SUSY. (*On stairs.*) Of course I can! I've been going there by myself for weeks.

MIKE. I'll get it much quicker.

SUSY. (*After hesitating.*) But the studio's locked. If anyone sees you go in . . .

MIKE. I'll be careful. Which is the key? (*Susy hesitates, then takes the keys from her purse, coming down stairs.*)

SUSY. The large one lets you in. One of the small ones opens the desk. You unlock the middle top drawer—and then they all spring open. But Mike . . . !

MIKE. Yes?

SUSY. You'll come back!

MIKE. Of course. Soon as I've got it.

SUSY. And bring it with you. We'll *dispose* of it *here*.

MIKE. I will. Where's his studio?

SUSY. 78 West Eighth Street. (*Mike repeats the address loud and clear [i.e. so at least one of them will remember it].*)

MIKE. I'll find it. (*She takes off coat and lays on back of settee.*)

SUSY. But please be careful . . . Carlino came back while you were gone.

MIKE. (*With faked surprise.*) He did? . . . But you didn't let him in?

SUSY. I had to. (*She laughs.*) You should have seen us! Carlino was at the door. The *safe was wide open*. The phone started ringing and then the doorbell and I could hardly tell which was which! (*Roat glares at Carlino.*)

MIKE. What did he want?

SUSY. Oh he just asked a lot of silly questions. And I could hear him searching for that doll all over the room—he even— (*She laughs.*) —he even looked in the *washing machine!* Can you imagine! But it's all right! (*Slowly.*) He now *thinks* it's in the *safe!* And he's going to get a warrant and have it drilled open. And by the time they've done *that*—there just won't be no doll—will there?

MIKE. There sure won't.

SUSY. Go on, Mike, and hurry!

MIKE. I will.

SUSY. And lock this door—and the street door as you go out.

MIKE. Okay.

SUSY. Good luck! (*Mike goes to top of stairs and opens hall door. The three men exit—Mike last—and closes the door—Susy listens to make sure they have gone. She then crosses to sink, finds a heavy utensil, feels until she finds the water pipe [which leads up the side of the wall] and bangs on it three times. After a few moments there are three muffled knocks on the pipe from Gloria. Susy then goes to the blackout and makes some arrangement whereby no one may open the blackout in the normal way: i.e. 1) If the blackout is a sliding shutter which is manipulated by means of a cranking handle [as it was in the Broadway Production] she simply pulls out the handle and hides it. 2) If the blackout consists of curtains manipulated by a hanging cord, Susy stands on stool, and ties a knot in the cord so that it is too high to reach and tucks it behind the curtain. As she finishes doing this there is a knock on the door.*) Who is it?

GLORIA. It's me. Gloria! (*Susy crosses and lets her in hall door.*)

SUSY. Lock the door, honey.

GLORIA. (*Locking it.*) Did you get my two signals?

SUSY. Yes! You were *wonderful!* Now quickly, *who* was it who went into that phone booth?

GLORIA. The last one was Sam's friend.

SUSY. Mr. Talman?

GLORIA. Yes.

SUSY. And before him?

GLORIA. The man with glasses.

SUSY. Who?

GLORIA. That man I thought was a detective.

SUSY. That's Mr. Roat.

GLORIA. And they just left the house with that police sergeant who was in here. They all went back to the Volkswagen. (*A pause.*) Susy—are Mr. Talman and Mr. Roat police detectives, too?

SUSY. They *may* be. Anyway I'm not taking any chances till Sam gets back. Do you know the Port Authority Bus Terminal?

GLORIA. The what?

SUSY. It's the—just ask for the biggest bus station in New York—I think it's near Forty-second Street.

GLORIA. Near Forty-second Street.

SUSY. Go out the back way and take the first taxi you can find. (*Handing Gloria her purse, Susy takes out the knife first.*) Here—take all the money in this—all of it. (*As Gloria takes out several dollar bills and puts the purse back in Susy's hands.*)

GLORIA. What do I do when I get to the bus place?

SUSY. Ask where the buses come in from Asbury Park—*Asbury Park*. Say that.

GLORIA. Asbury Park.

SUSY. Meet *every* bus that comes in from there. Just stay there all night if you have to. Sam will be on *one* of them. Can you do that?

GLORIA. Of course I can. What shall I tell him?

SUSY. *Everything.* And he will know what to do.

GLORIA. About the doll . . . ?

SUSY. About the doll and the three men and the Volkswagen. Everything you can think of. (*Gloria starts up the stairs then turns.*) Wait a minute. Before you go—can you find me some ammonia and some vegetable oil?

GLORIA. Where are they?

SUSY. (*She points to the kitchen shelves.*) Under the sink . . . and in that cabinet. (*As Gloria searches for the bottles, Susy goes to table, puts the knife down and feels for the vase of flowers. She carries it to the sink and holds the flowers, so they do not drop out.*) Ammonia.

GLORIA. (*Takes bottle from cupboard under sink.*) Got it.

SUSY. Pour some into this vase . . . quite a lot . . . watch out for your eyes. (*Gloria pours in some ammonia. They both wince at the smell.*)

GLORIA. Ugh! What's this for?

SUSY. For just in case. . . . Go on . . . a little more. Okay. Now a little oil on top of that . . . to stop it smelling. (*Gloria pours in some oil that she got from the wall cupboard over the stove.*) Now put those bottles away where you found them. (*As Gloria does what she is told.*) Now—where's the fuse box? Can you see it?

GLORIA. The what? (*From now on their speech and action become more and more rapid.*)

SUSY. (*Searching.*) There's a fuse box in the wall somewhere . . .

61

near the stairs I think. (*She puts out her hand.*) Take me to it. (*Gloria takes Susy's hand and leads her to the fuse box. Note: There are actually two fuse boxes—a large one and a small one just above it.*) Now go round the whole apartment turning on all the lights. Start in the bathroom. (*Gloria turns just before entering bedroom.*)

GLORIA. On—or off?

SUSY. (*Impatiently.*) On! . . . On!

GLORIA. (*A little hurt.*) Okay. Okay.

SUSY. I'm not mad at you, honey—just in an awful hurry. Those men are coming back here!

GLORIA. (*Calmly.*) That's okay, Susy—I'm not mad either. (*Gloria exits into bedroom.*)

SUSY. Is it dark outside yet?

GLORIA. (*Off.*) No—not quite.

SUSY. I wish it would hurry up. Close the drapes in the bedroom.

GLORIA. (*Calling off.*) I will. (*Pause.*) They just switched on the street lamps.

SUSY. Good. (*We hear Gloria closing the drapes in bedroom and then several lights go on in there—one after the other. Meanwhile Susy has opened the fuse box and is feeling for the [screw] fuses. Then Gloria enters from bedroom.*)

GLORIA. All on.

SUSY. In here too?

GLORIA. Yes.

SUSY. Good. Now—as I take out each fuse—tell me which light has gone *off.* Ready?

GLORIA. Yes. (*Gloria runs back into bedroom. As Susy unscrews each fuse and drops it into her zip purse, Gloria calls out:*) Bedroom . . . bathroom . . . all out in there . . . (*She enters.*) . . . ceiling . . . that one . . .

SUSY. *Which* one?

GLORIA. Sorry—on Sam's bench—it's just by you. (*Susy screws that fuse back in again.*)

SUSY. Now *that* one I want to keep . . . is it on again?

GLORIA. Yes. (*Susy unscrews the last fuse.*) Wall lights . . . that's all. Except the clock—

SUSY. Oh—pull the plug out.

GLORIA. Okay. (*Gloria unplugs electric clock. Susy now feels until she finds Sam's bench lamp.*)

SUSY. Now—don't be frightened, honey—I'm going to turn this one off for a second.

GLORIA. I won't be frightened. (*Susy turns off bench lamp at the lamp itself.*)

SUSY. Now—can you see anything at all?

GLORIA. No!

SUSY. Absolutely dark?

GLORIA. *Yes!* (*Susy moves away from the bench and waves her hand.*)

SUSY. Can you see me moving? Look very carefully.

GLORIA. Yes—*just.*

SUSY. (*Quite angrily.*) Then there *must* be a light from *somewhere*—where's it coming from?

GLORIA. From under the door at the top of the stairs.

SUSY. Hell! Okay—wait. (*Susy switches on the bench lamp.*) There's a broom in the stair closet. (*As Gloria gets it.*) Go into the hall, sweetheart, and smash every bulb in sight. Just go on until you can't see anything.

GLORIA. *Will do!* (*Gloria runs up the stairs and unlocks door and disappears L. Through the open door we can then see the light swinging as she strikes—once, twice and three times at the hall light. Then there is a bang and the light goes out. Another bang and the hall is dark. Gloria enters.*) All out! (*Susy immediately switches off bench lamp.*)

SUSY. Close the door. (*Gloria closes it.*) See anything now?

GLORIA. Nothing at all.

SUSY. All dark?

GLORIA. Yes! (*Susy switches on bench lamp. Gloria comes downstairs and returns broom to closet.*)

SUSY. Good! Off you go then—know what to do?

GLORIA. (*Running upstairs to door.*) Asbury Park. Tell Sam everything.

SUSY. . . . Lock that door and check that the street door is locked. Then go out the back way and run until you find a taxi.

GLORIA. Bye, Susy. (*She opens hall door.*)

SUSY. And, Honey . . . (*Willing her to succeed.*) I just don't know *anyone* who could do all this as well as you.

GLORIA. Oh boy I wish something like this would happen *every* day! (*Gloria exits, locking hall door. Susy stands still for a moment and listens. We hear the back door open and slam and Gloria run* ning out into the alley. *Susy remains still for a moment as though thinking hard:* "What else must I do?" *She goes to the table, finds the knife, knocks it on the floor, goes down on knees and finds it. She moves around for a moment as though wondering where to put it. Then she goes to the washing machine, opens it and hides the knife underneath the washing. As she closes the washer door . . .*

CURTAIN

END ACT II—SCENE 1

ACT II

Scene 2

TIME: *A few minutes later.*
ALTERATIONS TO SET: *None.*
ON RISE: *As before the room is lit only by the lamp on Sam's bench. Susy sits at the kitchen table . . . waiting and listening. The vase of flowers is in front of her, and a box of matches. She is smoking a cigarette.*
Susy stubs out cigarette, then suddenly she becomes very alert. She turns as though listening to a noise from the back door. We have heard nothing from that direction but she has. The door handle turns quietly as someone tries it. Then there is a quiet knock. Susy does not move nor answer. Then we hear Mike's voice calling quietly:

MIKE. (*Off.*) Susy. (*She does not reply. He calls louder and more urgently:*) Susy . . . there's something I must tell you. It's important. (*She does not move. Then we hear something being fitted in between the door and the lock and after some patient rattling the door opens and Mike enters. He returns a piece of celluloid to his pocket. He then closes the door [locked] and comes down the stairs. He is very angry. Susy does not rise.*)
SUSY. (*Calmly.*) Hello Mike . . . I was expecting you . . . did you get into the studio all right?
MIKE. As it happens—I did . . . no thanks to you. I don't know

whether you've ever been there *or not*—but there is *no desk*. (*Mike throws the bunch of three keys onto the floor.*)

SUSY. And no doll? (*Mike stares as Susy for several seconds.*)

MIKE. (*Quietly.*) How long have you known?

SUSY. About what?

MIKE. Me.

SUSY. (*As though to a friend.*) Now that's much better, Mike. Isn't it? Now we can talk like sensible people.

MIKE. (*Quietly.*) Where is it? (*A pause.*)

SUSY. You'll have to *buy* it.

MIKE. (*After a pause.*) Go on then—how much?

SUSY. Not money. I'll trade you—truth for truth. Let's start with Sam and Mrs. Roat—*true or false?*

MIKE. Do you know where it is? (*No reply.*) I can't trade if you *don't* know.

SUSY. I know.

MIKE. Here?

SUSY. How about Sam?

MIKE. If I tell you—can I have it right now?

SUSY. (*After a pause.*) In a few minutes—you *could*—yes.

MIKE. Then it *is* here.

SUSY. Well?

MIKE. Sam didn't kill that woman. He first met her at the airport *just like he told you.*

SUSY. So you aren't a policeman . . . nor is Sgt. Carlino.

MIKE. No.

SUSY. Have you ever met Sam?

MIKE. No. Is it in the safe?

SUSY. Who was she?

MIKE. I can't tell you that.

SUSY. Did you kill her?

MIKE. No.

SUSY. (*Quickly.*) Did *Mr. Roat?*

MIKE. (*After a pause.*) You don't have to know that either . . . in the safe?

SUSY. Yes . . . it's in the safe.

MIKE. The key?

SUSY. It's already unlocked.

MIKE. Thank you, Susy. (*Mike goes to the phone and dials a number. As he waits excitedly and then speaks, Susy remains per-*

fectly still and tries to hear the other end. *Mike, into phone.) It's here . . . yes . . . yes! Now!* May be your only chance. *(Note: this phone call is Mike telling Carlino to kill Roat as planned. See later. Mike hangs up and goes to safe. Susy waits until he reaches it and tries the handle of the safe. [It is locked.] Then she makes a dive for the phone and dials O.)*

SUSY. *(Very quickly into phone.)* This is 27B Grogan Street . . . *(But before she has said the word "Grogan" Mike has crossed quickly to phone and wrenched the cord out of the floor socket.)*

MIKE. That was just stupid—wasn't it? *(Susy doesn't answer. Mike, angrily.)* The key please! You said I could have it.

SUSY. *(Rises and backs away from him.)* I've hidden it. Very carefully. It's *somewhere* in this apartment.

MIKE. *(Following her.)* I'm not going to search for it. You're going to give it to me now.

SUSY. Then you'll have to *make* me give it to you. *(A pause. Mike's voice is cold as he does all he can to scare her.)*

MIKE. Don't think I couldn't.

SUSY. Then you'll have to hurt me *very* much . . . and I'm not so sure you can do that. *(He moves very slowly towards her.)*

MIKE. Then you don't know me very well.

SUSY. I think I do.

MIKE. You don't know me at all—do you?

SUSY. You can know some people very well—in a short time . . . you might be able to hurt me a little. But that won't be enough . . . *(There is a sudden and violent revving-up of a car from the alley outside. Then we hear a man shout and the sound of a trash can being knocked violently against the alley wall. Then the car revs off. Mike turns his full attention to this and for a few moments ignores Susy. A short pause as Mike's attention switches from what has just happened outside to Susy.)*

MIKE. *(Gently as though giving in.)* Perhaps you're right . . . maybe I just couldn't hurt you enough. *(A pause.)* But suppose there was a man who could . . . *(He watches her reaction. For the first time she begins to look frightened.)* . . . and suppose he was waiting right outside here . . . where he has been waiting all day . . . just for this. *(A pause.)* All I have to do is walk out of here and he'll come in.

SUSY. *(Raising her voice.)* Anything he does you'll be doing yourself. You'll never forget that.

66

MIKE. I won't be here. (*A pause.*) Have it your way then. (*He goes up the stairs.*)

SUSY. (*Shouting angrily.*) Go on then *get out!* You're worse than he is! (*Mike opens hall door and then turns.*)

MIKE. (*Desperately.*) But WHY? . . . How's Sam going to feel when he comes back here and finds you . . . ?

SUSY. (*Shouting violently.*) I *won't* give it to you! *Get out!* (*Mike looks down at her for a long moment. Then he closes the door quietly and comes down the stairs.*)

MIKE. (*Quiety.*) Okay, Susy—you win. (*Susy doesn't understand this and shouts violently again.*)

SUSY. Get out!—If you come near me . . . ! (*Mike halts and says quietly:*)

MIKE. It's all over, Susy. You can keep your damned doll. I guess you've earned it anyway . . . and you needn't be afraid of Mr. Roat any longer. Mr. Roat is dead.

SUSY. (*After a pause.*) Are you still lying?

MIKE. No more lies. I can't tell you much—who I am or who Carlino is . . . and we never knew who Mr. Roat was anyway. We only met him last night—but no more lying.

SUSY. You've killed him? (*As Mike talks he crosses, picks up phone from floor and returns it to table. During Mike's next speech, just for a moment, we can see a faint flicker of light under the hall door, i.e., as though someone has just entered the hall and struck a match.*)

MIKE. When Roat was in here doing his old man act—Carlino and I flipped a coin and he won. I can't tell you why we had to kill Roat but we did. Then the three of us agreed that—when I'd gotten the doll—Carlino would bring his car round to the back alley and pick up Roat and me. So as Mr. Roat walked round into the alley just now . . . a '58 Pontiac through the back of the head.

SUSY. You better go, Mike.

MIKE. How much are you going to tell about us?

SUSY. Will you leave Sam and me alone—always?

MIKE. That's a promise—we'll never meet again.

SUSY. Then I won't give you away.

MIKE. What about Sam?

SUSY. He'll do as I ask him. You see, I *am* grateful. It's rather like thanking someone for not pushing you under a bus—but you could have hurt me and you didn't.

MIKE. Goodbye, Susy. (*He turns to go.*)

SUSY. What will you do now?

MIKE. Run. I owe money to a Shylock and his boys are looking for me. That's why I had to do this. I'll just run and run—won't be the first time.

SUSY. There's a—it's not much but there's still that twenty-dollar bill at the back of the freezer—if that would help.

MIKE. We already took it—but thanks just the same. (*Susy puts out her hand.*)

SUSY. Goodbye then. (*As Mike takes her hand she puts her other hand up as though to feel his face, but he takes it gently with his other hand and pulls it down.*)

MIKE. (*Quietly.*) Uh—uh . . . no see—no tell. (*He turns and as he goes quietly up the stairs.*)

SUSY. Good luck. (*He opens the door. As he turns in the doorway to take one last look at Susy, he suddenly stiffens and falls down the whole flight of stairs, clutching at the railing. Susy calls, terrified.*) Mike! (*Roat enters and closes the hall door [i.e., locked]. He wears gloves. He wipes his knife and puts it away. He carries his zip bag. As he comes slowly down the stairs he says, quite mildly :*)

ROAT. Well Susy—now all the children have gone to bed—we can talk.

CURTAIN

END OF ACT II—SCENE 2

(*Author's Note: If preferred, Scene 3 may continue immediately, without a curtain. In this case Roat simply drags Mike into bedroom and action continues as described in Scene 3.*)

68

ACT II

SCENE 3

TIME: *A minute later.*

ALTERATIONS TO SET: *None.*

ON RISE: *We can just see Mike's legs disappearing into the bedroom as Roat drags his body in there. Susy is standing D. C. After a few moments Susy cautiously feels her way round the settee towards the stairway but just as she reaches for the railing Roat comes silently out of the bedroom and bars her way. She recoils and works her way backwards to where she was before. Roat goes upstairs and fixes a chain and padlock to door handle and railing.*

ROAT. I'm going to lock us in, Susy . . . so . . . *the dog it was that died!* Of course I knew they'd try and kill me the moment we had the doll. But when Carlino walked up to his car just now he saw it start up—all by itself—and drive straight at him. I couldn't resist switching on the light just to catch his expression . . . I don't think I've ever seen anyone look quite so surprised! So it's in the safe, is it? (*No reply from Susy. He comes down stairs.*) Take your time. At best Sam will just be arriving at St. Vincent's Hospital. You see, when his bus arrived at Asbury Park he was given a phone message which said you had had a slight accident and by the time they've kept him waiting around there I'll have finished. So will you give it to me now—please.

SUSY. I won't give it to you.

ROAT. I *won't* give it to you. I *won't* give it to you . . . you remind me of someone else who talked like that . . . only she said "I don't know where it is . . . I don't know—I don't know . . ." over and over again. (*Then from his zip bag he takes out a very lightweight chiffon scarf and turns and watches her.*) I've heard people say that before—only she was more stubborn . . . I don't know—I don't know. (*He flings the scarf into the air so it almost floats over her head. She recoils from it violently and as the scarf tangles in her fingers she backs away from it as though someone had handed her a snake. Finally it falls to the floor. He watches all this as though it was some kind of experiment. Quietly.*) Do you

frighten easily? . . . (*A pause.*) It's just in front of you on the floor. Would you pick it up, please . . . there's no need to be ashamed . . . everybody's frightened of *something.* (*Instead, Susy backs away—until she touches the table. Then, as he talks, she slowly maneuvers her way round, until she is close to the flower vase. As though his experiment has so far succeeded, he picks up the scarf himself. During the above dialogue he has taken from his zip bag a metal can [of gasoline] and now goes to the top of the stairs and sprinkles it all over the stair carpet and around the bedroom door and into the bedroom. When he comes out of bedroom he puts the can on top of the safe. During the above Susy feels around the table until she finds the matches and puts them into the pocket of her sweater. Roat, during above action.*) I have gasoline here. This place will go up like a matchbox . . . it's simply a question of whether you want to be outside in the street—or locked in there with Mike . . . won't you give it to me now?
SUSY. No.
ROAT. I won't give it to you—I don't know—I don't know . . . and then finally—as it *always* happens—something seemed to snap . . . and she told me everything she knew. As it happened she *didn't* know where it was but she told me *everything* she *could* . . . at last she *wanted* to help me . . . and like her *you* won't stop at that . . . when she'd answered all my questions—she went on —other things—little things that just *might* be useful to me . . . and then other things—things I didn't even *want* to know . . . little intimate things about herself and Mike and Carlino and I kept telling her—*that's enough*—I don't want to know any more—but she went on and on and on . . . (*Simply:*) and then she was dead. (*While he has been talking he has been moving closer and closer to her.*) I'm not going to ask you for it again, Susy . . . so when you *want* to give it to me—you have to tell me. (*No reply. She is still feeling the flowers. He moves even closer and says very gently:*) Then will you go in there? . . . Shall I help you? (*As he touches her lightly on the arm, she throws the vase and its contents into his face. His hands fly to his eyes. Susy makes a violent dash for the bench lamp and starts to move L. of the settee, knocking over a chair and stumbling. This gives Roat a chance to recover. He sees what she is aiming for and goes round the other side of the settee and reaches the lamp before her. But Susy has heard him move and changes direction and hurling herself across the room she reaches*

70

the light switch by the bedroom door. [Let us call this "the bedroom light switch."] Roat makes a frantic dash to get to her before she can switch it off but he is too late, and Susy switches the bench lamp off [from the bedroom light switch]. The stage is now completely dark. We now cannot hear Susy moving. But we hear Roat as he gropes for the bedroom light switch. When he switches on the bench lamp [from the bedroom light switch]—this is what we see: Susy has now moved across to the bench lamp and is feeling for it [i.e. in the dark—they have changed places—which is exactly what she intended]. We see her kick off her shoes. Then just as she touches the bench lamp Roat flicks out his knife and takes aim.) Don't touch it! *(As Susy lifts the lamp to smash it, Roat "throws" his knife and we see it stick and quiver in the back wall just above Susy's head [See Production Notes and diagram p. 88.] and a split second later she smashes the lamp against the wall.* Complete darkness again.)

[Author's Note: *During the following periods of complete blackout it is essential that the audience can hear what goes on but see nothing at all. In the Broadway production this was achieved satisfactorily by merely minimizing the theatre lighting out-front.] (We hear the sound of a key as Susy takes it out of bedroom door. Roat's first move is to the back wall to retrieve his knife. We hear him clumsily searching the wall. Then we hear Susy speak, she has now moved to the safe,* D. R.)

SUSY. *(Quietly.)* I have your knife, Mr. Roat. *(Neither speaks now for several seconds. Roat is standing perfectly still and his breathing gradually quietens until we cannot hear him at all. Then he strikes a match. He is still over by Sam's bench. Susy is by the safe and she has his knife in her hand.)*

ROAT. *(Very calmly.)* I can see you now, Susy . . . I have a whole box of matches . . . you're over by the safe. *(With her other hand she feels on the safe until she finds the bottle of gasoline. She then turns and goes straight for him. As he sees what she is about to do he shouts:)* No! *(He blows out the match.)* I've blown it out. It's out! *(Just before his match went out we saw Susy [aiming at his voice] start to souse him thoroughly with the gasoline. Once more in the darkness we hear him choke and splutter.)*

SUSY. Just try lighting a match *now!*

71

ROAT. I won't!

SUSY. (*She strikes a match and holds it out towards him.*) Throw your matches onto the floor . . . now! Or I'll set you on fire. (*He throws his box of matches on floor and she blows out her match.*)

ROAT. They're on the floor. (*Note: As Susy gradually regains command of the situation and then wins round after round she becomes calmer and gentler until, finally, she speaks rather like an experienced teacher talking to a rebellious child.*)

SUSY. Now stand perfectly still where you are . . . and listen. (*Silence for a few seconds, then we hear Roat start to tiptoe towards the stairs. Susy, sharply.*) Don't move! . . . However quietly you move I can hear you. (*He stops. Her voice now comes from the bedroom door.*) Now listen . . . go slowly to the bedroom door and walk so I can hear you . . . go on. (*We hear Roat start towards bedroom but he knocks into the side table.*)

ROAT. (*Frightened.*) I—I can't. I don't know where I am.

SUSY. (*As though to a child.*) Just find one of the walls and work your way around . . . it's not very difficult. (*We hear him cross to the bedroom door. He knocks on it to show he is there.*)

ROAT. I'm by the door. (*Susy's voice now comes from above the settee.*)

SUSY. (*Calmly.*) Now go inside . . . close the door and knock from the other side. (*We hear him feeling for the key in the lock.*) I have the key here.

ROAT. What are you going to do?

SUSY. Just go in there—close the door and knock. I'm going to lock you in . . . go on.

ROAT. (*From bedroom door.*) No. Let me stay in here. I won't move. I'll go and sit at the table . . . (*As he speaks we can now hear him going very quietly up the stairs. They creak as he mounts each step.*) . . . I'll keep knocking on the table so you'll know I'm there. . . . (*He suddenly makes a dive for the hall door but before he gets near enough Susy strikes a match. She is already up there ahead of him. She holds it out in front of her at arm's length. He stops dead on the stairs, screams sharply.*) No! Put it out! The gasoline! (*Holding the lighted match in one hand and his knife in the other Susy comes down the stairs after him as he backs away. As her match goes out we hear him fall down the last few stairs. Then in the darkness we hear him scramble for the table and he starts to beat on it loudly. Roat, in a panic.*) I'm at

72

the table and I'll keep tapping on it so you'll know exactly where I am. . . . (*Then we hear him move a chair as he sits.*) Now I'm sitting at the table. (*He starts tapping loudly on the table with his knuckles—a continuous tapping [but not in rhythm], but after several seconds he stops tapping.*)

SUSY. Keep tapping. (*He continues tapping. Neither speaks for several seconds.*)

ROAT. (*More quietly.*) I have to hand it to you . . . I don't know anyone who could have done this . . . you thought of *everything.*

SUSY. (*Gently.*) Just keep tapping. (*Roat continues tapping—as before—with intermittent knocks on the table—but during his next speech they change gradually into a more precise rhythm until he is finally beating a hard sharp slow rhythm which is also punctuating what he is saying. At the same time something sinister creeps back into his voice as if he has had an idea and is daring her to guess what it is.*)

ROAT. (*Continuing.*) . . . It's funny—when most people plan something (*Tap, tap, tap.*) . . . however clever they are (*Tap, tap.*) . . . there's always some little thing (*Tap.*) . . . they overlook . . . (*He stops tapping.*) but you, Susy . . .

SUSY. (*Sharply.*) Keep tapping! (*He does not tap any longer. She shouts:*) Keep tapping! (*Roat's voice is moving away from the table as he says:*)

ROAT. . . . You didn't forget anything . . . did you?! (*He opens the refrigerator, throwing a wide beam of light straight across at Susy who stands at the bottom of the stairs. [The refrigerator immediately starts its loud hum, which goes on and on.] Susy goes straight for the refrigerator as fast as she can with his knife held in front of her. But before she reaches it he snatches up a towel and loops it up over the hinge of the door so that when she slams it shut it only swings wide open again. She does this frantically several times. He stands back and watches her. Roat, very quietly.*) Won't it shut? (*She tries to lean against it but it won't quite shut and there is always at least a thin streak of light. In trying desperately to close it she drops the knife on the floor and Roat calmly flicks it just out of her reach with his foot. As she goes down on her knees to feel for it,*) So you see—it's all finished! . . . You can relax now, Susy. It's all over. (*He bends down and picks up his knife and says quietly:*) I have the knife. (*A pause.*)

Now get up and go over to where you were standing before . . . go on.

SUSY. (*Terrified.*) I'll give it to you . . . *I'll give you the doll* . . .

ROAT. No, no! Do as I say . . . (*She is now standing so as to be lit by light from refrigerator. At the same time he takes a chair and places it so that it holds the refrigerator door wide open [the refrigerator continues its loud hum]. He then goes to the sink and, as he talks, washes the gasoline from his clothes. Note: This is the only time he takes off his gloves and when he has finished drying himself he puts them on again.*) Back a bit . . . to your left . . . that's right . . . hands by your sides. (*A pause.*) Now—what was it you wanted to say?

SUSY. I'll give you the doll—if you'll just promise to go—and leave us alone.

ROAT. (*After a pause.*) You have to say . . . *please* may I give you the doll?

SUSY. Please may I give you the doll. (*A long pause, while he puts on his gloves etc.*)

ROAT. (*Quietly.*) You may. (*He watches her as she feels her way to the washing machine and opens it. As she searches inside her body masks [from him] what she is doing. She searches for several seconds and then brings out the doll. [We may or may not notice that she has slid the small kitchen knife up the sleeve of her sweater.] Roat is surprised to see where she had hidden the doll.*) You are clever, aren't you? . . . a little arrogant at times—but clever . . . now go and put it on the table. (*She takes it to the table.*) Now back to your place. (*She moves D. C. and stands there with back to audience and during what follows we must see her slide the knife out of her sleeve and hold it behind her back. Meanwhile Roat slits open the back of the doll and then tears it open pulling out several small bags of white powder. He fetches his zip bag and stuffs in the little bags. As he does this the musical doll starts to play. He collects all his things together and puts them with his zip bag at the bottom of the stairs. Then he puts on his raincoat. He is now ready to go. Finally he looks around until he sees his box of matches on the floor. He picks them up and rattles them [as though for Susy's benefit] and tosses them onto the top stair. When he has completed the above—he says mildly.*) Now may I have the key . . . to the bedroom? (*She takes the key from her pocket and gives it to him.*) And now—if you'll go into the bedroom please.

SUSY. (*Pleading like a child.*) You have what you want now— will you please go. I'll never give you away . . . if you'll just go.

ROAT. (*Mildly.*) I'd like to do that, Susy . . . but I have a rule that has to be obeyed—you know the one I mean? (*He is now moving closer to her.*) . . . That clever, arrogant girls have to be punished. . . .

SUSY. No!

ROAT. I'm only doing what you were going to do to me. I'm going to lock you in there . . . go on. (*He puts his hand lightly on her elbow but she shakes him off and turning starts to go obediently to the bedroom. He follows just behind her.*) That's right. But you mustn't shout. If I hear you call for help, I'll set fire to the stairs. Then no one will be able to help you until the firemen arrive and by that time . . . (*As she reaches the doorway he suddenly tries to push her inside but she turns and catches hold of his coat. At first he does not see the knife in her other hand as she stabs at him once, twice, three times [always just missing]. Then he sees it and tries to back away but she still holds onto his coat and won't let go. In the struggle they have now turned around so that as he tries to get away from her he backs into the bedroom and she puts her head down and goes in after him stabbing violently and wildly. They remain in there for at least ten seconds. Then she almost falls in through the door, stumbling and dropping the knife, she feels around for it frantically but cannot find it on the floor. She then gives up searching and rushes in the wrong direction smashing violently into the safe and almost knocking herself out. She recovers and starts trying to find her bearings. She stumbles up the stairs and tries to open the door but the chain prevents her. She then turns and stumbles down the stairs to look for the knife. As she reaches the bottom of the stairs, Roat suddenly lunges violently into the room [hitting the door hard as he passes it] and falls several feet into the room grabbing at Susy. Susy screams and falls and he grabs at her leg just missing it. He sees knife on floor and grabs it. Susy crawls towards refrigerator. She flings the chair aside and tries to close it but the towel still keeps it springing open again. Then Roat stabs his knife into the floor ahead of him and pulls himself along the floor towards Susy. As he does this again and again, sliding along the floor like a reptile, she freezes with*

75

fear and listens to him coming nearer and nearer. Then she makes a wild effort to find the electric cord on the R. side of the refrigerator. She begins to shout for help.)

SUSY. Help me! Help me! (*But her voice seems half-strangled and hardly any noise comes out. As he slides nearer Roat says:)*

ROAT. I'll help you, Susy. (*She goes to the other side of the refrigerator, i.e., behind its open swinging door. She searches for the cord that side but her way is barred by the dish rack and as she tears her way to the cord, dishes and silver fly in all directions. At last she finds it and tugs at it but nothing happens. Roat reaches the refrigerator and hauls himself up, using the inside trays like a ladder. Then he steadies himself against the swinging door and raising his knife hurls himself and the door at Susy. Just as he does this she gives a final tug and the light goes out and the refrigerator stops humming. Complete darkness again and silence in the room. Then immediately we hear footsteps and shouting. There is banging on the hall door and then it breaks open with a splintering crash. Patrolman One enters followed by Patrolman Two. They flash their lights around the room until one halts on Roat's body. Sam runs in calling:)*

SAM. Susy! (*Note: The action and speeches by the Patrolmen and Sam must be rapid and should, to some extent, overlap.)*

PATROLMAN TWO. (*On landing.*) You better stay out of here, Mr. Hendrix! (*Sam rushes past him and down the stairs and into the bedroom.*)

SAM. (*Calling off.*) Susy!

PATROLMAN TWO. (*Down the stairs after him.*) Mr. Hendrix! (*Meanwhile Patrolman One has come down the stairs with his flashlight on, and has gone over to Roat. Note: Susy has been knocked out and is lying behind the refrigerator door which is held wide open by Roat's body and neither we nor they can see her yet. Roat is in a grotesque position, apparently dead, one sleeve is caught in the refrigerator shelf so he is half hanging by one arm and his weight is so placed as to hold the refrigerator door wide open, completely masking Susy.*) That's one of 'em. I'm going in there. (*Indicates bedroom. Sam now enters from the bedroom and runs up the stairs and out of the door off L. He passes Patrolman Two in the bedroom doorway.*)

SAM. She's not here! I'll check upstairs. (*Patrolman One is examining Roat.*)

PATROLMAN ONE. He's still bleeding—may stand a chance. (*Patrolman Two draws his gun and enters the bedroom. We hear him kick open the bathroom door and open a closet. Meanwhile Patrolman One looks round for the phone, finds it, picks it up. After rattling the phone he hangs up. Patrolman Two enters from bedroom [having returned his gun to holster].*)

PATROLMAN TWO. There's a D.O.A. in there—looks like a knifing.

PATROLMAN ONE. Phone's dead . . . first aid bag and ambulance . . . (*As Patrolman One says this he is moving Roat away from the refrigerator so as to attend to him. He does not see the door start to close, revealing Susy for the first time. She is now conscious but dazed and gets up and begins to feel her way,* D. L. *Suddenly noticing her, Patrolman Two whips out his gun and goes down on one knee.*)

PATROLMAN TWO. (*Shouts.*) Watch it! (*Patrolman One turns sharply drawing his gun, so they are now both aiming their guns and flashlights straight at Susy. As though in reply she strikes a match and holds it straight out in front of her. Then she stands there quite still, arm outstretched, holding the lighted match as if it was her last and only means of protection. Gloria appears in the hall door and looks down. For a moment the two patrolmen simply stare at Susy, completely bewildered as to who she is and what she is doing. Then seeing she is unarmed they put away their guns but keep their flashlights on her.*)

PATROLMAN ONE. (*Gently.*) Put that match out! (*Gloria runs down the stairs and pushes her way between the two men. Takes Susy's hand and gently blows out the match.*)

GLORIA. Susy—are you all right? . . . It's *me*—we're back. (*Patrolman One goes to Susy to help her out of the room.*)

PATROLMAN ONE. (*Gently.*) Okay, lady—let's get out of here, shall we? (*But Gloria pushes him aside.*)

GLORIA. Leave her alone! *Both* of you. She can manage by herself. (*Gloria takes Susy by the hand and leads her to the settee, which is the nearest thing Susy can recognize. Gloria then leaves her to herself and then, as she backs away from Susy, she picks up a fallen chair, moves another chair, moves a side table, etc., as though she has only one thing in mind—: to clear the way for Susy so she can get up the stairs in her usual way and without help. During this the two patrolmen keep their flashlights on Susy* and Gloria so as to light their way. *As Gloria goes* backwards *up the stairs [watching Susy all the time] she says:*) You see . . . she can manage . . . she'll be all right. (*As Susy is halfway up the stairs Sam enters from* L. *He starts to come down and then, sensing the situation, he steps back and waits for her.*)

SAM. (*Quietly.*) Susy. (*Then he holds out his hand and lets her grope around until she finds it. As she touches it everyone is very still.*)

CURTAIN

END OF PLAY

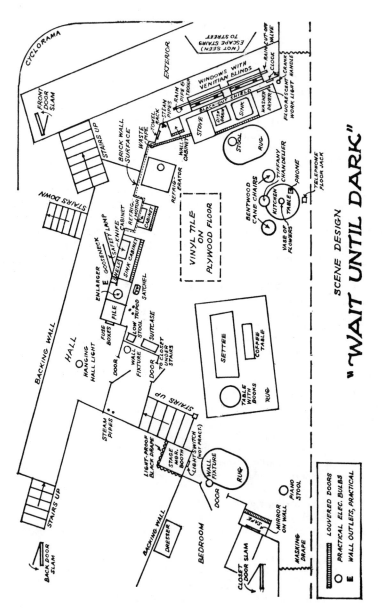

"WAIT UNTIL DARK"

SCENE DESIGN

PROPERTY PLOT

Act I—*Scene* 1

Bedroom (off R.)
Dresser with 4 drawers
  On top:
    9" x 12" folding photo album with wedding picture of Sam & Susy
    Paper-back "pocket" book (Sam I-2)
    Men's billfold (Sam I-2)
    Miscellaneous: bottles, jars, comb, brush, mirror (unbreakable)
Traverse rod with drapes (closed)
Vacuum cleaner
Laundry (pile of wrinkled sheets)
Suitcase, old with center key lock
  Inside:
    10 letters and envelopes; typewritten with rubber band around them
    4 red or manilla file folders
Closet door slam
Crash box and bulb to break (each performance) (II-1)
Hooks for costumes:
    1. Roat's raincoat: double of Susy's—bloodstained (may not be used)
    2. Sam's raincoat and suit jacket
    3. Susy's raincoat and shoulder purse (Set Act I intermission)
Coffee cup, empty (Carlino I-3)

Back Door (off U. R.)
Back door slam

Prop Table (off U. C.)
Brass knuckles (Carlino)
*Razor blade (wrapped in cardboard) (Mike I-1)
Handkerchief (Carlino) (Personal)
Airline zipper, shoulder bag (Roat I-1) with:
  *2 pieces of Kleenex
  *2 bank packages of money—$500 each
  *1 metal skeleton type key (to closet door)
  "Geraldine"—a gravity knife with ivory statue handle—lethal looking
  *1 pair plastic disposable gloves
  1 empty baby food jar, with screw top
4 Men's wristwatches (Sam, Mike, Carlino, Roat)
Carpet—old, faded, dilapidated about 6' x 5' (Roat)
*Key to front door (practical snap lock) (Susy)

Gold cigarette case and lighter (with cigarettes) (Roat I-1)

*2 cigarettes in soft package (Sam I-2)

Men's work apron (Sam I-2)

Rubber glove (left hand, for a right-handed Sam I-2)

Handkerchief (Roat, Sr. I-3)

Child's eye-glasses, nude plastic frame (Gloria) (Personal)

Package addressed to M. Talman, Phoenix, Arizona (Mike I-2)

Man's black umbrella (Roat, Sr. I-2)

*Matches: (Susy and Roat II-3)

   Box safety matches

   Book matches

   Large kitchen (any surface) matches

Brown leather brief case (Roat, Jr. I-3)

Men's rimless eye glasses (Roat, Jr. I-3)

Grey fedora (Roat, Jr. I-3) (Costume)

Black felt hat (Carlino) SET II–1

Large brown grocery bag with doll (should be well wrinkled so it does not make any noise when being handled) (Gloria II-1)

   The doll used in the N. Y. production was 22″ long and 6″ wide. It had silver hair and a red taffeta dress. It was stuffed with soft material and was constructed so that it could fold at the hips (in half). (II-1)

Dope doll:

   The second or "dope doll" looked exactly the same as the first one, but had been remade so that it could be ripped apart at each performance. It was seamed at the chest and back (so the head could be removed) with Valcro, and down the back (so that the doll could be completely opened) with Valcro.

3-4 cubes of heroin:

   Inside the dope doll were 4 cardboard cubes 1″ x 1″ x 3″. The second doll with the heroin is placed in the washing machine at the Intermission.

Plastic glove (left hand for a right-handed Carlino) (I-3, II-1)

A water spraying device—or some provision for wetting the actor's costumes, as it is raining throughout much of the action of the play. (Only if rain effect used.)

*1 pair black-plastic framed wrap-around ski-sun glasses with thin shaded viewing strip (Roat II-1)

Bicycle lock—metal, snap-lock type—long enough to reach around door knob and through railing. About 3 feet (opened). Or chain and lock. (Roat II-2)

*2 spiral backed pocket sized pads (3″ x 5″) (Mike, Carlino) WA 4-5309 written in both of them. (Roat I-1)

*2 pencils (Roat I-1)

Quart size wide-mouth metal gasoline can with screw top—2/3 filled
   with water (Roat II-2)
White crepe 12″ square scarf (Roat II-2)
Plastic playing card for opening door lock (Mike II-2)
3 flashlights (each policeman carries one spare flashlight) (II-3)
1 torch ("Sportsman"—RAY-O-VAC) Flashlight (II-3)
2 Revolvers (II-3)
Slip of paper, with address (Roat I-3)
Gloves (Roat I-3, II-1, 2, 3)

Front Door (platform u. l. off)
Front door slam
Shoulder purse (Susy) (Costume)
   with: key to front door
           several dollar bills
Regulation blind stick (white with red base and metal tip) (Susy)
1 box safety matches
1 skeleton door key (Susy II-3)
Stick to bang on off stage pipe (Gloria's answering knocks)
Off d. l.
Thermos bottle—pint size
Silver table knife
2 slices ham
Piece of waxed paper (to wrap sandwich)
Empty bread-loaf wrapper
Brown sandwich bag—wrinkled (noiseless)
Metal ashtray—SET II–2
Lit cigaret (in ashtray)—SET II–2
Grocery list, and five dollar bill

Arranged so that Susy
can easily pick them
up and carry them off
stage.

Living Room d. r., r. and c. stage
Safe with key lock 22′-6″ x 1′-2″ x 3′ x 9″—louvered door facade
   On top:
      Metal ashtray with smoke effect.
      The smoke effect must last about 1 minute, and was accomplished
   in the N. Y. production by using smoke "bombs," sulphur tipped
   kitchen matches, and bits of torn paper. There was a hole drilled
   in the top of the safe, about 2″ diam. Eight 1/8″ holes were also
   drilled in the bottom of the ashtray. Over each ashtray hole, place
   the head of a match (plus an inch of the wooden match stick). On
   top of the matches, place two smoke cartridges (about an inch and
   a half long) each containing a kitchen match. Between the "bombs"
   and on top of the matches place 4 or 5 small pieces of paper,
   twisted in the center ("butterflies") so they do not smother the

flame, but feed it until the "bombs" are ignited. Over the contents of the ashtray, a piece of wire mesh screen is needed so the bombs cannot pop out of the ashtray. When Susy goes off into the bedroom, a strong up-right flame (such as can be obtained by using a butane lighter) should be held under the hole in the safe, by someone in the bedroom.

Piano stool

Rug—oval 3' x 4'-10" in front of bedroom door

Carpet—on stairs and landing

Broom—in closet under the stairs

Settee—4'-6" x 1'-9"—bentwood—carved, open-work back and arms
   Cushion—throw pillow (12" x 12")

Table—fruit wood, swivel base, 2 tiers
   On top:
     Metal ashtray
     1st shelf: *books* to fill (about 40)
     2nd shelf: 4 magazines—stack of 6 *Books*

Coffee table (in front of sofa)
   Metal ashtray (on s. r. stool)

Rug—8'-9" x 6'-0" (under settee, table and coffee table)

Photo Alcove (u. c.)—(r. to l.)

2 fuse boxes with a total of 6 fuses (in wall, over file cabinet)

Suitcase (2' x 18") next to stairway: empty (for Sam to pack equipment)

Stool (9" to 12" rise) in corner of stair landing (this is to enable Susy to open the Hall door without having to climb up the stairs)

Metal file cabinet—snap lock, key opening, (not practical)
   3 drawers:
     Top drawer—manilla folders, envelopes (dressing)
     Middle drawer—stuffed file folders, negatives, etc. (dressing)
     Bottom drawer—cardboard cigar box with:
       (a) small key on large paper clip with tag labeled "small suitcase" (i.e. the one in bedroom)
       (b) 3 keys on a ring; 1 large, 2 small
       (c) 3 keys on a (different) ring—that could conceivably open the safe
       (d) 10 assorted keys (dressing)

Cabinet—1 open shelf, 2 drawers
   On top:
     Photographic enlarger (practical)—plugged in, switch in "off" position
   In front:
     Tripod: pointed metal spikes on the ends of the leg extensions that

might be used for out-door photographing. This is leaning against the file.

(next to enlarger) *Enamel dish* (white, open 6″ deep—that might have been a storage drawer in refrigerator)—zip cord and switch for enlarger is in this dish.

Under enlarger nose is a sheet of white cardboard, (18″ x 24″) angled at 30° and an 8″ x 10″ black and white photo of Susy (turned blank side up—i.e., undeveloped picture)

Open shelf under enlarger:

Plastic cover for enlarger

On floor in front of cabinet:

Shoulder satchel brown canvas, zipper closure (empty—for Sam to pack his equipment)

Sink with cabinet underneath: faucet and 2′ length of hose (not pract.)

In sink:

3 developing trays

Double of Geraldine (hidden under lip of center tray)

Hanging on cabinet door knob:

Camera case

Inside cabinet—1st shelf:

2 strobelights

10 packages of rolls of film

1 camera case

Inside cabinet—2nd shelf:

1 bottle of liquor 1/2 filled

Shelf over sink:

Goose neck lamp with 150 watt silver-tipped bulb—practical

Safe lamp (practical—plugs in enlarger outlet) unit with orange colored light that Sam can have on while he is working

Wall over shelf:

Double *electrical outlet* in which are plugged the enlarger and the safe lamp. (practical)

Double door cabinet hanging on wall that houses trick knife spring release (when Roat throws the knife at Susy in II–3)

Photo of Marines

Cabinet with two doors:

On L. side of cabinet is a piece of sand paper or some rough surface on which Roat may strike his match in II-3. This cabinet may be filled with canned goods, dishes, glasses but there is a false back which serves to mask a shelf for the refrigerator motor. This sound was achieved by attaching a household metal-blade fan and a cup-cake tin (loosely) with piano wire in 4 places to the wire frame (fan guard). The fan was then plugged into a "variac" dimmer, and thus a loud or low rumble of the refrigerator could be provided and remotely.

Kitchen (u. l. to d. l.)

Refrigerator: temperature dial turned to "on" position

In freezer:

Key to filing cabinet

$20.00 bill

Freezer compartment is covered with heavy frost. (Spray "snow" from an aerosol can will adhere and looks very much like refrigerator frost.)

2nd shelf (under the freezer) 500 watt "quartz light" (practical). In the N.Y. production, this bulb was housed in a metal box (3 sided)—that was painted white to match the interior of the refrigerator. The open side of the box, which faced the audience was half masked by a replica of a milk carton which was made of metal. This prevented the bulb from glaring directly into the audience, and directed a shaft of light all across stage. Once the angle of light had been determined, the milk carton was attached to the metal box containing the bulb, and the fixture was fastened to the side and to the shelf of the refrigerator.

Jar of mayonnaise next to light

1/2 pound of sliced cheese, wrapped in waxed paper (next to mayonnaise)

4th shelf: photographer's power pack. (not practical)

N.B. Any electrical cord or cable that might appear in the area of the refrigerator must be very carefully concealed, lest it be construed (by the audience) as "the cord to the refrigerator."

Along l. set wall—from u. to d.

On wall next to refrigerator: Towel rack with towel yellow, thick terry cloth and dish towel

Corner cabinet:

Over cabinet:

Wall cabinet:

Bottom shelf:

Jar of mustard (practical)

Bottle of vegetable oil (yellow food coloring and water)

Stove:

Left rear burner: coffee pot, percolator type, metal, top should be fastened on. No inside parts or breakable or loose attachments. (Gloria throws these)

Right front burner: metal frying pan (Gloria throws this)

Sink:
On drain board:
Plastic dish drainer with detachable silver (drainer) holder
In drainer:
Heavy plastic handled serving fork, or some instrument Susy can bang pipes with
Unbreakable (plastic) dishes, glasses, plastic bread basket, sharp knife** (Gloria throws these)
In silver holder:
6 pieces assorted flatware
1 sharp (paring) knife
In sink: faucets—one is practical
Cabinet under: garbage pail with brown paper bag insert. In the N.Y. production, a large, light weight brown plastic wastebasket was used. A light-weight paper bag was used that had a wide opening and could be rolled down over the side of the basket, concealing anything from view that is under the garbage bag.
Crumpled envelopes, including Sam's used airline ticket, in pail.
Shelf in u. cabinet door: bottle of ammonia. (The ammonia used was water and powdered cream.)
In front of sink:
30" wooden stool
Oval rug 4'-10" x 3'-0"
Washer-dryer—front opening and quiet snap closure (empty)
On top:
Wicker laundry basket (D. end of washer. The basket should not cover the whole top of machine, as the garbage can should be able to be placed next to it)
In basket:
Misc. laundry (towels, "t" shirts, shorts, etc.)
Lady's nightgown
Lady's apron
Shelf over washer: (On pegboard) glass apothecary jar labeled "SUGAR" and containing lump sugar
On pegboard:
Clock (practical) no glass, hands of clock should operate from a screw on the face, so that the time the clock shows can be quickly changed
Electrical outlet in which the clock is plugged
Above pegboard:
Two windows with Venetian blinds. The cords that operate the blinds must be reached by someone standing on the floor.

o. of washer: *Crank* that operates counter-weighted blackout shield. The crank must detach easily.

**The *sharp knife* which is later used to stab Roat was a silver plated piece of flatware. This blade caught the light, and appeared very lethal-looking, while being safe for an actor to use in violent play. The handle was wrapped with black-plastic electrical tape.

Table: (L. of c.)

This should be a sturdily built table, with thick metal base, and should have a washable surface. The table used in the N.Y. production had a marbleized, glazed top.

On the table:

Telephone with a *cord* that reaches under leg of table.

Vase with *flowers**

The vase should be low (4″) and unbreakable. The flowers were small plastic buds with short stems.

Salt and pepper shakers

Ashtray: "beanbag" or other unbreakable material

*Pad of paper (3″ x 5″)

*Pencil

2 chairs:

In the N.Y. production, these matched the settee—bentwood with cane seats. Light, but sturdy construction.

PRODUCTION NOTES

1. The prop items accompanied by an asterisk indicate necessity for frequent replacement.

2. The *floor* of the entire set was vinyl tile on 3/4" plywood backing; but in any case, it must be water-proof.

3. The entire set must be "light tight." It was necessary in the N.Y. production to operate back stage in almost complete blackout, during the "blackout" or dimly lit scenes on stage.

4. The Stage Manager's booth was the only place from which the whole set could be viewed. This was accomplished by having two of the pictures—which decorated the walls at the stairs and adjacent to the bedroom door wall—made of scrim. These pictures were backed with a light proof material (removable) so that when necessary, a work light could be used in the booth. Also, the entire booth was surrounded with this light proof material.

5. Five light bulbs are broken during each performance.
   In bedroom, when Susy breaks the lamp (1).
   In the hall—(3) are broken simultaneously with Gloria's swinging of the broom.
   In the photo alcove. When Susy smashes the gooseneck lamp, the base of the lamp smashes a bulb (preset at intermission) in the corner of one of the developing trays in the sink.

6. The platform in the hall area was covered with canvas, and half of it planked with "shimmed up" (about 1/4") x 1" x 12" lumber. This enabled the audience to hear approaching footsteps when necessary, or when the opposite effect of an actor approaching silently was desired, he would walk on the canvas portion of the platform.

7. The *trick knife* was housed inside a wooden cabinet hanging on the wall in the photo alcove. It is a double of Roat's "Geraldine," except the blade is extended (inside the cabinet). Welded to the blade is a metal "U"—shaped guard which (when the knife is released, makes a thudding noise against the off stage side of the cabinet door. The knife rides forward and backward by a piece of clothes rope attached to the end of the "blade" in a wooden track. Two heavy rubber bands (or elasticized tubing) are put on either side of the "U." On

a warning signal the rope is pulled back, putting spring tension on the rubber bands. When Roat "throws" his knife, the rope-pull is released, and the knife shoots out through a hole in the cabinet door. When Susy smashes the gooseneck, during the blackout which follows, the knife is withdrawn into the cabinet.

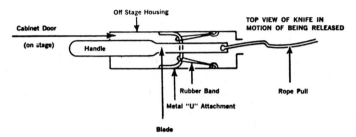

8. (Author's Note: In the Broadway production there was a mechanical device to produce the effect of rain on the windows. This was for atmosphere and *not* essential to the play and could be dispensed with.)

NEW PLAYS

- **SMASH by Jeffrey Hatcher.** Based on the novel, AN UNSOCIAL SOCIALIST by George Bernard Shaw, the story centers on a millionaire Socialist who leaves his bride on their wedding day because he fears his passion for her will get in the way of his plans to overthrow the British government. *"SMASH is witty, cunning, intelligent, and skillful."* –Seattle Weekly. *"SMASH is a wonderfully high-style British comedy of manners that evokes the world of Shaw's high-minded heroes and heroines, but shaped by a post modern sensibility."* –Seattle Herald. [5M, 5W] ISBN: 0-8222-1553-5

- **PRIVATE EYES by Steven Dietz.** A comedy of suspicion in which nothing is ever quite what it seems. *"Steven Dietz's ... Pirandellian smooch to the mercurial nature of theatrical illusion and romantic truth, Dietz's spiraling structure and breathless pacing provide enough of an oxygen rush to revive any moribund audience member ... Dietz's mastery of playmaking ... is cause for kudos."* –The Village Voice. *"The cleverest and most artful piece presented at the 21st annual [Humana] festival was PRIVATE EYES by writer-director Steven Dietz."* –The Chicago Tribune. [3M, 2W] ISBN: 0-8222-1619-1

- **DIMLY PERCEIVED THREATS TO THE SYSTEM by Jon Klein.** Reality and fantasy overlap with hilarious results as this unforgettable family attempts to survive the nineties. *"Here's a play whose point about fractured families goes to the heart, mind -- and ears."* –The Washington Post. *" ... an end-of-the millennium comedy about a family on the verge of a nervous breakdown ... Trenchant and hilarious ... "* –The Baltimore Sun. [2M, 4W] ISBN: 0-8222-1677-9

- **HONOUR by Joanna Murray-Smith.** In a series of intense confrontations, a wife, husband, lover and daughter negotiate the forces of passion, lust, history, responsibility and honour. *"Tight, crackling dialogue (usually played out in punchy verbal duels) captures characters unable to deal with emotions ... Murray-Smith effectively places her characters in situations that strip away pretense."* –Variety. *"HONOUR might just capture a few honors of its own."* –Time Out Magazine. [1M, 3W] ISBN: 0-8222-1683-3

- **NINE ARMENIANS by Leslie Ayvazian.** A revealing portrait of three generations of an Armenian-American family. *" ... Ayvazian's obvious personal exploration ... is evocative, and her picture of an American Life colored nostalgically by an increasingly alien ethnic tradition, is persuasively embedded into a script of a certain supple grace ... "* –The NY Post. *"... NINE ARMENIANS is a warm, likable work that benefits from ... Ayvazian's clear-headed insight into the dynamics of a close-knit family ... "* –Variety. [5M, 5W] ISBN: 0-8222-1602-7

- **PSYCHOPATHIA SEXUALIS by John Patrick Shanley.** Fetishes and psychiatry abound in this scathing comedy about a man and his father's argyle socks. *"John Patrick Shanley's new play, PSYCHOPATHIA SEXUALIS is ... perfectly poised between daffy comedy and believable human neurosis which Shanley combines so well ... "* –The LA Times. *"John Patrick Shanley's PSYCHOPATHIA SEXUALIS is a salty boulevard comedy with a bittersweet theme ... "* –New York Magazine. *"A tour de force of witty, barbed dialogue."* –Variety. [3M, 2W] ISBN: 0-8222-1615-9

DRAMATISTS PLAY SERVICE, INC.
440 Park Avenue South, New York, NY 10016 212-683-8960 Fax 212-213-1539
postmaster@dramatists.com www.dramatists.com

NEW PLAYS

• **A QUESTION OF MERCY by David Rabe.** The Obie Award-winning playwright probes the sensitive and controversial issue of doctor-assisted suicide in the age of AIDS in this poignant drama. *"There are many devastating ironies in Mr. Rabe's beautifully considered, piercingly clear-eyed work ... " –The NY Times. "With unsettling candor and disturbing insight, the play arouses pity and understanding of a troubling subject ... Rabe's provocative tale is an affirmation of dignity that rings clear and true." –Variety.* [6M, 1W] ISBN: 0-8222-1643-4

• **A DOLL'S HOUSE by Henrik Ibsen, adapted by Frank McGuinness. Winner of the 1997 Tony Award for best revival.** *"New, raw, gut-twisting and gripping. Easily the hottest drama this season." –USA Today. "Bold, brilliant and alive." –The Wall Street Journal. "A thunderclap of an evening that takes your breath away." –Time. "The stuff of Broadway legend." –Associated Press.* [4M, 4W, 2 boys] ISBN: 0-8222-1636-1

• **THE WAITING ROOM by Lisa Loomer.** Three women from different centuries meet in a doctor's waiting room in this dark comedy about the timeless quest for beauty -- and its cost. *" ... THE WAITING ROOM ... is a bold, risky melange of conflicting elements that is ... terrifically moving ... There's no resisting the fierce emotional pull of the play." – The NY Times. " ... one of the high points of this year's Off-Broadway season ... THE WAITING ROOM is well worth a visit." –Back Stage.* [7M, 4W, flexible casting] ISBN: 0-8222-1594-2

• **MR. PETERS' CONNECTIONS by Arthur Miller.** Mr. Miller describes the protagonist as existing in a dream-like state when the mind is "freed to roam from real memories to conjectures, from trivialities to tragic insights, from terror of death to glorying in one's being alive." With this memory play, the Tony Award and Pulitzer Prize-winner reaffirms his stature as the world's foremost dramatist. *" ... a cross between Joycean stream-of-consciousness and Strindberg's dream plays, sweetened with a dose of William Saroyan's philosophical whimsy ... CONNECTIONS is most intriguing ... Miller scholars will surely find many connections of their own to make between this work and the author's earlier plays." –The NY Times.* [5M, 3W] ISBN: 0-8222-1687-6

• **THE STEWARD OF CHRISTENDOM by Sebastian Barry.** A freely imagined portrait of the author's great-grandfather, the last Chief Superintendent of the Dublin Metropolitan Police. *"MAGNIFICENT ... the cool, elegiac eye of James Joyce's THE DEAD; the bleak absurdity of Samuel Beckett's lost, primal characters; the cosmic anger of KING LEAR ..." –The NY Times. "Sebastian Barry's compassionate imaging of an ancestor he never knew is among the most poignant onstage displays of humanity in recent memory." –Variety.* [5M, 4W] ISBN: 0-8222-1609-4

• **SYMPATHETIC MAGIC by Lanford Wilson. Winner of the 1997 Obie for best play.** The mysteries of the universe, and of human and artistic creation, are explored in this award-winning play. *"Lanford Wilson's idiosyncratic SYMPATHETIC MAGIC is his BEST PLAY YET ... the rare play you WANT ... chock-full of ideas, incidents, witty or poetic lines, scientific and philosophical argument ... you'll find your intellectual faculties racing." – New York Magazine. "The script is like a fully notated score, next to which most new plays are cursory lead sheets." –The Village Voice.* [5M, 3W] ISBN: 0-8222-1630-2

DRAMATISTS PLAY SERVICE, INC.
440 Park Avenue South, New York, NY 10016 212-683-8960 Fax 212-213-1539
postmaster@dramatists.com www.dramatists.com